WATERSTONE'S
AUTUMN BOOK SAMPLER

WATERSTONE'S
AUTUMN BOOK
SAMPLER

Published by Random House 2004

2 4 6 8 10 9 7 5 3 1

First published in Great Britain in 2004

Random House, 20 Vauxhall Bridge Road,
London SW1V 2SA

Random House Australia (Pty) Limited
20 Alfred Street, Milsons Point, Sydney,
New South Wales 2061, Australia

Random House New Zealand Limited
18 Poland Road, Glenfield,
Auckland 10, New Zealand

Random House (Pty) Limited
Endulini, 5A Jubilee Road, Parktown 2193, South Africa

The Random House Group Limited Reg. No. 954009
www.randomhouse.co.uk/vintage

A CIP catalogue record for this book
is available from the British Library

ISBN 0 09 948267 3

Papers used by Random House are natural, recyclable products made from
wood grown in sustainable forests. The manufacturing processes conform to
the environmental regulations of the country of origin

Printed and bound in Great Britain by
Bookmarque Ltd, Croydon, Surrey

INTRODUCTION

I first came across Ruth Rendell's eerily strange books on moving to live in London. Her novel *Live Flesh* had just been published. As I read I quickly realised that I had moved to the exact area of the city she was describing. In a feeling that must be recognised by readers of Ian Rankin living in Edinburgh, or of Graham Hurley in Portsmouth, I found that Rendell's fictional version of north London, and my real-life one, blurred slightly until it wasn't difficult to imagine the twisted thoughts moving behind each blank face on the bus, or the warped goings-on behind every respectable front door.

I soon read book after book – there is no more regularly entertaining writer around. Rendell has continued to write about London in many of her novels, imbuing its streets and suburbs with menace, making the safe and familiar disquieting and dark. Try reading her novels *The Rottweiler* or *The Keys to the Street* and then thinking of Marylebone and Regent's Park in the same way as before, for instance. Her best-known books are the lengthy series of Inspector Wexford novels, successfully filmed for television over the last twenty years. But for her very many fans Rendell is at her peak when writing on the psychology of crime and delving deep into the minds of her characters – whether victim or persecutor. Hardly conventional whodunits, books like *A Demon in My View*, *The Tree of Hands* or *A Judgement in Stone* are minor nightmares for the reader, entry-points to a world of madness and murder. Full of suspense, we continue to read and watch as, inevitably, the tiny moving pebble sets off the avalanche.

No less a crime writer than Patricia Cornwell has described Ruth Rendell as the best in the business. Certainly among current British crime writers only P. D. James can compare in terms of the consistently high quality of her novels over many years: Rendell has been writing for no less than forty. If you haven't yet tried her books, you could start now with her latest novel *Thirteen Steps Down*, an extract from which is one of the highlights of the Waterstone's Autumn Book sampler that you are holding in your hands.

It can be difficult to choose when faced with a Waterstone's full of great new books. We've taken some of that problem away with this book of extracts from twelve of the best novels and non-fiction books being published this autumn. Dip in and see what suits you. Waterstone's booksellers who have already read and enjoyed the featured books introduce many of the extracts. We're pretty sure that you will enjoy them too. Among the highlights of our selection are the new novels by Kate Atkinson, Carl Hiaasen and David Lodge.

A real favourite of mine is Tim Moore's new book *Spanish Steps*. Every publisher is desperate to discover "the new Bill Bryson", and the man himself has cornered the market in funny travel writing so successfully that such desperation is no surprise. Tim Moore doesn't need any such comparison. *Spanish Steps* takes us on a journey to Spain's pilgrim city of Santiago de Compostela, by ass, naturally enough. There are plenty of laughs here, and more still in William Cook's *Goodbye Again*, a collection of the best scripts of Peter Cook and Dudley Moore. If, like Pete, you have nothing against Dud's left leg, start here.

Or if history is more your thing have a look at Max Arthur's *Forgotten Voices of the Second World War*. Compiled from the archives of the Imperial War Museum, this tells the story of the war using first-hand testimonials from the men who were there, ordinary soldiers from all combatant nations giving their personal recollections from six years of war. A very powerful and moving book.

So get browsing – I'm sure you'll enjoy our choice.

Martin Higgs, Waterstone's Literary Editor

FORGOTTEN VOICES OF THE SECOND WORLD WAR

BY MAX ARTHUR

Following the phenomenal success of *Forgotten Voices of the Great War*, which has already sold over a third of a million copies, I am delighted to say the sequel, *Forgotten Voices of the Second World War* matches the power and poetry of its predecessor. The often deeply moving personal accounts span the outbreak of war to the dropping of the atomic bomb on Nagasaki. The range is wide and diverse and includes children in the Blitz, soldiers on the beaches of Dunkirk, Dieppe and D-Day as well as those involved in the fierce fighting in North Africa, Italy and the sweltering jungles of Burma.

There are also tremendous accounts from the Royal Navy and Fighter and Bomber Command as well as those who waited or worked on the Home Front. In all, a vast and rich tapestry of emotions, that only war can bring out.

Max Arthur

£19.99
ISBN: 0091897343
Published October 2004

THE BATTLE OF BRITAIN

By summer 1940 a German invasion across the Channel was imminent. France had been conquered and Hitler's next thought was to invade Britain. The bulk of his troops and war material had to be conveyed by sea and in order to achieve this, he had to have air superiority. The destruction of Fighter Command was the essential prerequisite to the invasion of Britain. For Fighter Command, all possible resources were harnessed into building more aircraft, training more fighter pilots to defend the vital radar stations and key airfields on Britain's south coast. Their task was to make sure that the air superiority Hitler needed would never be achieved. Throughout the summer, from the first air raids in July to the final postponement of Operation Sealion on 17 September, Hurricanes and Spitfires were in action day in, day out. The pilots, many of them flying their first sorties, engaged the fighters of the Luftwaffe and the bombers they escorted, in dogfights over the south of England. The pilots and ground crews, exhausted, depleted and stretched to the limits of their endurance knew the desperate importance of their continuing battle. Only in September, when raids were diverted away from airfields to targets in London, was it certain that the tide had been turned and that the invasion would not take place.

Frederick William Winterbotham
Air Staff Department, Secret Intelligence Service
I think the most important signal we had through ULTRA, right at the beginning of the Battle of Britain, was Goering

establishing his strategy with his commanders. He told them that they were to fly over Britain and bring the whole of the Royal Air Force up to battle, because only in that way could it be destroyed in the time they had.

That was the key for Dowding – to fight the battle with very small units every time they came over – gradually wearing them down and always having aeroplanes to send up.

Raymond Charles Cooper
Boy in south of England
I was excited we were going to fight the Germans – I was fourteen at the time. We were near two squadrons – we used to count them out and count them back in, so we used to know how many were missing. I used to do that every day during the Battle of Britain. I saw so many dogfights during that time – some planes would come quite low and be forced down, and I saw some crash into the hills near my village and some fall into the sea.

Alec Ingle
Flying Officer, 605 Squadron
The first flight you made in the morning, you would get a sinking feeling in the pit of your stomach, until you saw the enemy and the minute you'd made your first interception, for the rest of that day it didn't matter what happened. The adrenalin was flowing and certainly, as far as I remembered, it flowed in reasonable quantity. Once you pressed your gun button, you could take on the complete Luftwaffe. That's the reaction I had to it.

Frederick Gash
Sergeant, 264 Squadron
We felt we had to stop the Germans if they tried to invade. I did talk to several of my 264 friends and comrades and colleagues about that. 'What're we going to do if the Germans do get here?' And most of them said, 'We've got to stop them from getting here – so why talk about what are we going to do if they get here? We've just got to stop them.'

James A Goodson
American Sergeant Pilot, 43 Squadron
Once you got used to the Spitfire, you loved it. It became part of you. It was like pulling on a tight pair of jeans, and it was a delight to fly. I used to smoke a cigar sometimes – against all rules and regulations – and if I dropped my cigar lighter, instead of groping around on the floor, I would move the stick a fraction of an inch, and the Spitfire would roll over, and I would catch the lighter as it came down from the floor. That was the kind of plane it was. Everyone had a love affair with the Spitfire.

Even the Germans got to respect it. I remember Peter Townsend went to see one of the German pilots whom he had shot down, close to the base. The German pilot said to him, 'I'm very glad to meet the Spitfire pilot who shot me down.' And Peter said, 'No, no – I was flying a Hurricane. I'm a Hurricane pilot.' The German kept arguing with him, and Peter kept saying, 'No – you were shot down by a Hurricane.' The German pilot said, 'Would you do me a favour? If you ever talk to any other Luftwaffe pilots, please tell them I was shot down by a Spitfire.'

Tony Bartley
Pilot Officer, 92 Squadron
We did five sorties a day. We never stopped – we just went. You went to your dispersal hut half an hour before dawn, but when the tannoy said scramble, you scrambled. You went up and you fought all day long until the sun went down. Whether it be three, four, five missions a day – you just fought and fought and fought. At the end of the day we got off the airfield, because they used to bomb us at night, so we would go down to the White Hart at Brasted and drink beer.

Al Deere
New Zealander, Flight Lieutenant, 54 Squadron
We were frightened. On the way out there was an awful gut fear. When you sighted them it really was – it was quite a frightening sight. But once you got into combat there wasn't

time to be frightened. But we were frightened – of course we were – the whole bloody time. But if you're in combat, you're so keen to get the other guy and, if you like, save your own skin, that your adrenalin's pumping and there's no room for fright.

I've often wondered why there weren't more collisions. There were probably more than we knew about, because if somebody collided, you didn't know about it. There was, in the initial engagement, a danger of collision. I collided with a 109 because we were both trying to come at each other head on. The closing speed was such that neither of us could get out of the way and we collided. I crashed in Kent on fire – he went into the sea.

Rosemary Horstmann
Sergeant, WAAF, based at Hawkinge
It was very dramatic, because several of the girls who were working with us had boyfriends who were pilots, so they would find themselves monitoring a battle in which their brothers and fiancés were fighting, and we were writing down what the German pilots were saying – things like, 'I've got him,' or 'He's down!' Sometimes you would hear people screaming.

Roland Beamont
Flying Officer, 87 Squadron
I was back on his tail, ready for another burst. It was then that I could see that he had his undercarriage down, and that he was streaming coolant. He started to sideslip fairly violently, and he did another roll – this time with his wheels down, and then a diving turn towards the ground. I thought either he was going to go in, or he was aiming for a forced landing. Obviously he was a very capable pilot.

Eventually he went in rather hard, to land in a field, buckling his undercarriage. He slid on his belly across the field and ended up at the far end, near a hedge. I dived around after him and saw him lift his canopy sideways, opening the cockpit. He jumped out, off the wing and lay flat on the ground. I wondered if he thought his aeroplane was going to blow up – and then I realised he might think I was going to strafe him on the ground. Of course the thought hadn't occurred to me.

George Herman Bennions
Pilot Officer, 41 Squadron
On 29 July, the first aircraft that shot at me, I ducked out of the way, but unfortunately it had hit my port wing and damaged the flaps and the undercarriage and all the guns. I managed to make Manston, but as I was coming in to land, the aircraft seemed perfectly alright as far as I was concerned. When I got near the ground, I put my flaps down, but only one flap went down, which was rather disastrous, because the aircraft slewed all over the place. Fortunately I'd left it until I was almost on the ground anyway. I'd pumped my under-carriage down, but what I didn't know was that one tyre had been blown off, and one leg damaged, and the flaps damaged – so when I hit the ground, the aircraft just spun across the aerodrome, like a Catherine wheel. I came to rest completely bewildered, not having the faintest idea what had happened – but very relieved to find I was still in one piece.

Geoffrey Page
Flying Officer, 52 Squadron
All these things, which looked like lethal electric light bulbs, kept flashing by, then finally there was a big bang and the aircraft exploded. The beauty of the Royal Air Force training came to my rescue and I instinctively reached for the harness and slid the hood back. I rolled the aircraft on to its back, kicked back the control column so the aircraft pointed its nose upwards, but as I was upside down, I popped out like a cork out of a toy gun.

I stupidly wasn't wearing any gloves, so my hands got a terrible burning, and face as well. My mouth and nose were saved by my gasmask. I found myself tumbling head over heels through space. I remember seeing my right arm and extending it, making myself pull the metal ring of the ripcord on my parachute – and that was agony. It was like an electric shock through my burnt hand. Again, haven't a choice, because, if you don't, the parachute won't open.

Fortunately, my parachute wasn't on fire. I then took stock of the situation, and noticed a funny thing had happened. My left shoe and my trousers had been blown off completely by the explosion. I was almost naked from the waist downwards. Then I could hear the fight all around me, and it took me about ten minutes to float down into the water.

I had various problems to deal with. First of all, I had to get rid of my parachute, but you had to turn this metal disk on your stomach. You turn it through ninety degrees and then give it a hard thump – but it was difficult because I was badly burnt. Then the parachute was on top of me, so I was really inside a tent with the cords trapping me like an octopus's tentacles. I knew I had to get it away quickly, otherwise I would sink. Again, desperation comes into the issue, so you do turn it, and you do thump it.

The next thing was to blow up my life jacket. I got hold of the rubber tube over my left shoulder, but when I blew into it, all I got was a lot of bubbles. It had been burnt right through. My face was swelling up at this point, and my eyesight was bad because my swollen eyelids were closing up. The distant view of England, which I could see a few miles away was a bit blurred, but I started vaguely in the right direction.

Then a happy thought came to my mind, and I remembered that in my jacket pocket I had a brandy flask that my dear mother had given me – which I had filled with brandy just as an emergency measure. I thought that this probably qualified as an emergency, so I rolled on my back. This was a painful process, but I got it out and held it between my wrists and undid the screw cap with my teeth. I thought, 'Well, life is going to feel a bit better.' But as I lifted it up to take a swig, a dirty big wave came along and the whole lot went to the bottom of the Channel. I was a bit annoyed about that, but there was nothing else for it, so I continued swimming.

I heard, rather than saw the boat. There were two men in it, and they kept asking me questions. By this time I had been swimming for half an hour, and I was fed up with the whole affair, so when they asked me if I was a Jerry, I'm afraid I let loose with every rude four-letter word that I could think of, and that immediately assured them that I was an RAF officer. They picked me out of the water, and took me to the big ship, where the captain dressed my burns and gave me a cup of tea. Then the Margate lifeboat came out and took me in to transfer me to Margate hospital.

For the first time for an hour or more, I was able to laugh, because waiting on the quayside was the Mayor, dressed in his top hat and tails, saying, 'Welcome to Margate'. When you'd been in an air fight an hour before, and then there's a chap in top and tails, it is two different worlds. As it happened, it was the beginning of grouse shooting that day, 12 August. There was a certain irony in that.

Geoffrey Page
Pilot Officer, 56 Squadron
Morale was tremendous, because the facts of life were, we would be flying many times during they day, having taken off in the darkness, and then, as the dawn came up, we'd fly to a forward base such as Manston or Hawkinge or Rochford – and then we'd be at readiness all through the day. Then in the evening, just as the light was beginning to fail, we'd fly back to our base at North Weald. Then there'd be a mad rush to get down to the local tavern before the pubs closed. Don't forget, we were all nineteen, twenty, twenty-one years of age. We were just overgrown schoolboys.

In all squadrons, fighter or bomber, during the war, there were commissioned officers and there were non-commissioned officers of sergeant rank. But while we were lying around our aircraft or in the air, there was no differentiation between ranks at all. I always felt it was a little unfair that after a hard day's fighting and you landed, one lot of us – the commissioned officers, we would go off to the officers' mess, and the sergeants would go off to the sergeants' mess. I think men who take an equal risk, you know, should live the same way.

Roland Beamont
Flying Officer, 87 Squadron

On a scramble on 15 August, the controller said, 'Bandits now twenty miles ahead of you. You should see them directly ahead.' Almost immediately the clear sky ahead started to turn into a mass of little black dots. Our CO continued to lead us straight towards it. I just had time to think, 'I wonder what sort of tactic he's going to employ. Is he going to turn up-sun and try and dive at them, or go round to the right and come in behind. What's he going to do?' While I thought that, it was quite apparent he wasn't going to do anything. He bored straight on into the middle of this lot until we seemed to be going into the biggest formation of aeroplanes you ever saw. Then his voice came on the radio and said, 'Target ahead. Come on, chaps, let's surround them.' Just nine of us!

I fired at a Ju 87 at point-blank range, and I hit it. I don't know what happened to it. But I could see my tracers going into it. Then I came under attack from directly ahead and below. It turned out to be a Me 110, doing a zoom climb straight up at me, firing as he came. He missed me. I rolled away from him straight behind another of his mates, another 110. I fired a long burst at him and his port engine stopped and started to stream smoke and fire, and I pulled away from that.

Bob Doe
Pilot Officer, 234 Squadron

On 15 August we were ordered up to Middle Wallop. We flew up there, but I was feeling very strange, in the sense that everything was distant – we hadn't been involved – it wasn't real. We landed on the grass airfield, we were put into a lorry, and halfway up to the mess, they bombed the airfield. One of the hangars was hit and a WAAF was killed in a trench. Up to that moment, we had been seeing the war from a spectator's point of view.

A bit later that day, we were scrambled over Swanage. I really had the worst inferiority complex at that time. I felt I was the worst pilot in the squadron, and I was convinced I would not survive that trip.

We took off and formed up into four Vics of three in sections astern – which is the stupidest formation you could possibly fly in. There's only one person looking round, everyone else is formatting. We patrolled up and down the sun, which again, is a stupid way of flying. At one point, we turned back down-sun to find we were only nine strong. We had lost three – our rear section had disappeared, one killed and the other two shot down. Then, all of a sudden, we found ourselves in the middle of a gaggle of Messerschmitt 110s and 109s. God knows how we got there – we just landed in the middle of them. I was flying No 2 to Pat Hughes, who turned off after a 110, gave him a quick squirt, then turned on his side and pulled away. But it didn't look quite right to me, so I formed on the 110, got quite close to it, and kept on firing until he went down into the sea. This was the second time I'd used my guns. The first was into the sea to try them out. I thought, this is something! I'm not dead, and I've done something! That feeling was really fantastic. I followed him down, pulled up from the sea, and another 110 overshot me from behind. I just closed on him and shot him down.

I shot two down without really knowing anything. I realised on the way home that I'd been so lucky, it was ridiculous. So I started to do some thinking. In fact, I went to bed early that night, and I stayed in bed just thinking. I realised that you're usually shot down from behind – so what do you do if you see bullets coming past you from behind? I worked out that, whatever I did, I must go down – straight down – because if you tried to roll or anything, you stayed in the bullet path for longer, and if you pulled up you were a sitting target. So I drilled it into my head that if I saw anything coming past me from behind, I would just hit the stick. I wouldn't think – just hit it.

The following day we met a load of 109s high up over the Isle of Wight, and I found one on his own. I settled down on him. Now, although I'd shot two down the day before, I was not certain about shooting. I couldn't trust my judgement and distance, and I couldn't trust my shooting. So I aimed above him at first, then below, and eventually I shot him down. But I had been so involved, that I hadn't seen another 109 behind me. Fortunately Pat Hughes had spotted it and shot it off my tail. I was dead lucky.

Douglas Hamilton Grice
Pilot Officer, 32 Squadron, dispersal at Hawkinge
It was 15 August – I was weaving like mad, looking right, left, centre, up, down – and mostly back – when suddenly, out of the corner of my eye, I saw a flash over my left wrist. The next moment, the cockpit was full of flames. The heat was enormous, and I'd done two things absolutely instinctively. My left hand had gone to the handle of the hood, my right hand had gone to the pin of my harness, and I was pulling with both hands. The next moment I was out in the open air.

There I was, falling away – and I did actually remember my parachute drill, which was to wait before pulling the rip-cord for two or three seconds. I pulled it, and there was a jerk – and there I was, floating down under a marvellous canopy, about a couple of miles inland. I could look down and see the land, and I thought, 'Well, at least I won't be going into the sea.' Well, very shortly after that, I was over the coast – and a few minutes later, I was a mile out to sea – and a few minutes after that, I was two miles out to sea. Well, before that, I'd taken my helmet off and dropped it, and that gave rise to a moment of immense panic. I actually watched my helmet drop from, I suppose, twelve or thirteen thousand feet, until it disappeared from view. I suddenly realised how high I was, and how much space there was between my toes and the ground. So I hung on to my straps like mad.

Jean Mills
British Auxiliary Air Force – plotter and tracer at Duxford, on edge of 12 Group
We were all pretty young – girls of only nineteen or twenty – when we got assigned to Duxford, and for a lot of us it was the first time we'd been away from home, so we were laughing

and joking, because it seemed like an adventure. Suddenly we reached the brow of a hill and we could see Duxford, stretching out in front of us. It was a beautiful sunny day. As we looked, we could see that something had happened. There were lots of planes – one plane seemed to hover and was nose-diving to the ground with smoke trails rising. The noise of our chatter stopped instantaneously and the mood changed. We realised it wasn't a great lark and that we were in for serious business. We were reminded of this because the pilot who was killed had an Alsatian, which kept roaming the camp looking for him. It was very sad.

Harold Bird-Wilson
Flying Officer, 17 Squadron
I was both worried and frightened at times. We were praying for bad weather – probably the only time anybody in England prayed for that! Somehow during the battle we had beautiful weather – sunshine and blue skies most of the time – and we did pray very hard. Fatigue broke into a chap's mentality in most peculiar ways. My chaps had the jitters and facial twitches. I had nightmares and used to wake up in the dispersal hut about twenty-five yards from my aircraft.

Frank Carey
Flight Lieutenant, 43 Squadron
Altogether I did about a hundred sorties in the Battle of Britain – from early July until 18 August. The most I did was six sorties in a day – roughly about an hour to an hour-and-a-half each one.

On one of those sorties I nursed a plane back from out in the Channel. The pilot got a glycol leak – it comes out in little white puffs that get more and more frequent. I flew alongside and said, 'You stay there as long as that thing will take you back to land. Don't worry, it's all right.' I don't know what he was suffering in the cockpit, mind you. His cockpit was open and it must have been pretty hot. When it was no longer a puff but a regular little stream, he couldn't stand it any longer and got out. I followed him down and spotted him in the sea. I circled and radioed for help until I ran out of fuel. He was never picked up. I can only suppose he got tangled up and pulled down by the parachute. When he went into the sea he was only about a mile-and-a-half off Selsey Bill. We didn't have any air sea rescue then. The Germans did. They used to fly rescue seaplanes even right along the English coast.

Air fighting is a very detached sort of warfare being fought, as it were, between machines with the human factor very much submerged in 'tin box'. Once in a while for a few fleeting seconds when someone bales out, one can suddenly be aware that humans are actually involved but, as the parachute descends, machines quickly regain the centre of the stage once more.

On one particular sortie from Wick, however, the human angle predominated for quite a while. The formation in which I was flying came upon a rather lonely Heinkel 111 way out in the North Sea, which we naturally proceeded to deal with. After a few shots, a fire was seen to start in the fuselage and the flight commander immediately ordered us to stop attacking it. The enemy aircraft turned back towards Wick and we escorted it on its way with me in close formation on its port side where the fire was. Being only a few feet away from the Heinkel it was all too easy to become sympathetically associated with the crew's frantic efforts to control the fire and I even began to wish that I could jump across and help them. I suddenly converted from an anxious desire to destroy them to an even greater anxiety that they survive. We had got within a few miles of the coast and had really begun to hope that they would make it, when we were all outraged to see a Hurricane from another squadron sweep in from behind and without a single thought about us all around, poured a long burst of fire into the Heinkel which more or less blew up in our faces and crashed into the sea without any survivors.

It was all I could do to prevent myself from spinning round and having a crack at the Hurricane in response to its action. I felt a sense of personal loss as I stared at the wreckage on the water.

Bob Doe
Pilot Officer, 234 Squadron

On 18 August they sent a very formidable force over the Southampton area. We had three sorties that day. I got one on the first, one on the second, and damaged one on the third.

We were so confident at that time. There was no doubt in our minds. We knew we weren't going to lose. It never, ever entered our minds that we could lose. I suppose, in retrospect, we were bloody stupid, but it never entered our minds that we could possibly lose this war.

Then we had a new CO posted in, and he decided to come as my No. 2 on a scramble. We found a lone Ju 88 over Winchester. Well, I had a go at it; he had a go at it – no effect. So I got behind it, got as close as I could, and filled it with bullets. He hit me through the main spar, then stopped firing and went into the ground. When we landed back at base, the new CO, very keen, wanted to go and have a look at the Ju 88. It had crashed in a field very close to Middle Wallop. I'm now very sorry I went to see it, because someone informed me that every aircrew helmet had bullet holes in it, and that brought everything home to me.

I had to fly the Spitfire down to Hamble for repair. It was a lovely warm day, with interceptions going on overhead all the time. The foreman of the place invited me home to lunch, and his wife started talking to me. Suddenly, for the first time, I realised that ordinary people in the street knew what we were doing, and that they admired us. She was saying things that made me blush. It really was quite something. I hadn't been aware of it – it hadn't entered my mind. People could see what was happening.

Jean Mills
Battle of Britain plotter

From the little rooms, the little wireless and radar rooms behind the controller, we could hear the crackling voices of the pilots come back, and although we had headsets on and the work was quite intensive and required a lot of concentration, we used to manage to ease one earphone off so we could hear what was going on, and then we could listen out for 'Tally ho', which meant they'd sighted the enemy, and then you could hear them talking to each other, like, 'Look out, Blue Two, bandits to your right.' And things like that, which seemed to bring it right into the room. There was an indescribable tension about the whole thing. When there was something going on, the atmosphere was electric. We were all rooting for our boys to come back. They were very much our pigeon.

Peter Brothers
Flight Lieutenant, 32 Squadron, dispersal at Hawkinge

Having got engaged one day I pressed the gun button and nothing happened at all, because the guns hadn't been reloaded. On landing back, I had the armourer in the office, drew my pistol, and said, 'I'll shoot you if you ever do that again.' But I was tired.

It was all fairly intense, but the waiting around at base was the hardest part. We'd sleep, play mahjong or read. When we were 'scrambled', one of our chaps would run to his aircraft, be violently sick, and then jump into his aircraft and be off. Your adrenalin really got going once that bell went. We all swore we'd never have a telephone at home after the war – because as soon as the telephone rang you'd all automatically be at the ready. Then you'd hear, 'No, corporal so-and-so has just gone to get his lunch,' and you'd all relax again. It would either be that or, '32 Squadron scramble 18,000 feet over Ashford,' and off you'd go.

After we returned from an operation, the Intelligence Officer would want all the details. We weren't all that interested, it was over, finished. But he needed the information. We'd tell him, but we could be scrambled in the middle of telling him something. During one of the raids on Dover, I'd shot down a Stuka and then gone into Hawkinge to refuel and rearm. I didn't even get out of the aircraft. They were rearming the aircraft and there was a chap standing on the wing in front of me, pumping fuel into the tank. The battle was still going on up above and, as we watched, a Spitfire shot

16

down a 109, and the pilot baled out. The airman who was refuelling me said, 'Got him!' And then, when the pilot's parachute opened, he turned to me with a look of utter disgust on his face and said, 'Oh, the jammy bastard!' As soon as they'd finished I was off again, back into the battle. But it was rather amusing. I got a 109 later on that day.

Ray Holmes
Sergeant, 504 Squadron
We built up a sort of synthetic hate against them, which was a bit artificial. I wanted to shoot an aeroplane down, but I didn't want to shoot a German down. I really did not. We did hear stories of Germans shooting our fellows in parachutes, and we used to think that was pretty horrible – but we weren't sure whether it was true or not. I know I had an experience of a German aircrew getting draped over my own wing – he bailed out of a bomber and got caught on my wing with his parachute, and I was jolly careful to get him off as easily and as quickly as I could, manoeuvring the aeroplane and shaking him off. And I was very glad when I heard he'd dropped down in Kennington Oval safely. So I had no feeling of wanting to kill that fellow personally.

Geoffrey Page
Flying Officer, 52 Squadron
After being shot down on 12 August, I spent a few days in Margate hospital and then I was taken up to the Royal Masonic Hospital in London, and then later on I found myself in Sir Archibald MacIndoe, the plastic surgeon's hospital in East Grinstead, where I spent two years undergoing plastic surgery. And from the six of us who started it, there've been about seven hundred through that hospital who've become members of the Guinea Pig Club. We thought, when we were allowed to get out of bed and walk a few yards, there was a little hut, and we said, 'Why don't we form a little club in there, where we can have a glass of beer and get away from the ward for half an hour or so?'

George Herman Bennions
Pilot Officer, 41 Squadron

I was very concerned and very upset. I was annoyed at myself for having been shot down so decisively, and I felt terribly isolated. I couldn't see or hear very well, and so I couldn't recognize people. I felt so very sorry for myself, which is not a good situation for anybody. I felt so deflated, that half of my life had been taken, and half wasn't worth bothering with. It was, I think, the worst period of my life, but you get over it.

There was one person in particular who put me on a much more even footing. He had been shot down by a Hurricane. He had sent a message to go and see him. I was on crutches at the time, and I managed to get over there with a hell of a lot of struggle and self-pity. As I opened the door in Ward 3, I saw what I can only describe now as the most horrifying thing I have ever seen in my life. This chap had been really badly burnt. His hair was burnt off, his eyebrows and his eyelids. You could just see his staring eyes, with only two holes in his face. His nose and lips were also badly burnt. Then I looked down, and saw that his hands and feet were burnt. I got through the door on my crutches with a struggle, and then this chap started propelling a wheelchair down the ward. Halfway down, he picked up the back of a chair with his teeth – and it was then that I noticed how badly his lips were burnt. Then he brought this chair down the ward and threw it alongside me and said, 'Have a seat, old boy.' It was then that I cried – and I thought, 'What have I got to complain about?' From then on, everything fell into place.

Brian Kingcombe
Flight Lieutenant, 92 Squadron

It was the most enjoyable part of the war. It sounds perhaps callous – I don't know – but it was enormously exciting and tremendous fun. And we had every advantage – to begin with, we were flying over our own territory, and this was a huge moral advantage. Because first of all, it gives you a reason for being there – because when you're over your own homeland, defending your own homeland, it gets the adrenalin going.

Jean Mills
British Auxiliary Air Force – plotter and tracer
I remember coming on for a night shift and seeing a great glow in the south east, like the biggest sunset you ever saw, and we said to the guard, 'What's that?' and he said, 'Oh, that's London burning.' That was the first time, really, that I felt it in the pit of my stomach.

Peter Brothers
Flight Lieutenant, 257 Squadron
The sporadic raids went on into December, then they reverted to 109s carrying bombs. Our squadron had moved from Martlesham Heath to North Weald. The winter was coming and clearly there was not going to be an invasion. The Battle of Britain had been won.

CASE HISTORIES

BY KATE ATKINSON

Kate Atkinson's dazzling first novel, *Behind the Scenes at the Museum*, was chosen as the 1995 Whitbread Book of the Year. Her subsequent publications confirm her reputation as an important writer, known for her wonderfully wry sense of humour, quirky characters, exquisite evocations of place (York in *Behind the Scenes . . .*, a fictional English suburb in *Human Croquet*, Dundee in *Emotionally Weird*), and her ability to mirror life in all its beauty and sordidness in plots full-to-bursting (Shakespeare and Dickens both come to mind) with secrets, lies, murders, disappearances, switched identities and thrilling narrative twists.

Atkinson frames her fourth novel, *Case Histories*, as a detective story. Set in Cambridge, it introduces displaced northerner Jackson Brodie as an investigator who, since leaving his position as Police Inspector and setting up his own agency, hasn't had, or wanted, a case more demanding (or less dull) than keeping tabs on the occasional cheating spouse or searching for missing cats.

But during the course of a sweltering Cambridge summer he's confronted with three important new cases. The first involves newly-found evidence in the 1972 disappearance, from her own backyard, of three-year-old Olivia Land. The second requires him to revisit the 1994 murder, in broad daylight by an apparent stranger, of gap-year student Laura Wyre. The third case involves tracing Tanya Fletcher, who, after her mother's murder of her father in 1979, was taken into foster care. In addition to these, a fourth, older, case emerges gradually and painfully from Jackson's own history.

Like Atkinson's previous three novels, *Case Histories* teems with satire and allusion, beautiful writing and virtuosic set pieces. While not shrinking from the devastation at the heart of things, it's delightfully funny. More proof that the sublimely talented Kate Atkinson is one of Britain's most exciting novelists!

**Recommended by Mary Dubberly,
Waterstone's Ludgate Circus London**

£16.99
ISBN: 0385607997
Published September 2004

Jackson switched on the radio and listened to the reassuring voice of Jenni Murray on *Woman's Hour*. He lit a new cigarette from the stub of the old one because he had run out of matches, and faced with a choice between chain-smoking or abstinence he'd taken the former option because it felt like there was enough abstinence in his life already. If he got the cigarette lighter on the dashboard fixed he wouldn't have to smoke his way through the packet but there were a lot of other things that needed fixing on the car and the cigarette lighter wasn't high on the list. Jackson drove a black Alfa Romeo 156 which he'd bought second-hand four years ago for £13,000 and was now probably worth less than the Emmelle Freedom mountain bike he had just given his daughter for her eighth birthday (with the proviso that she didn't cycle on the road until she was at least forty).

When he'd come home with the Alfa Romeo, his wife had taken one dismissive look at it and said, 'You bought a policeman's car then.' Four years ago Josie was driving her own Polo and was still married to Jackson, now she was living with a bearded English lecturer and driving his Volvo V70 with a 'Child on Board' sign in the rear window, testifying both to the permanence of their relationship and the smug git's need to show the world that he was protecting another man's child. Jackson hated those signs.

He was a born-again smoker, only starting up again six

months ago. Jackson hadn't touched a cigarette for fifteen years and now it was as if he'd never been off them. And for no reason. 'Just like that,' he said, doing an unenthusiastic Tommy Cooper impression to his reflection in the rear-view mirror. Of course it wasn't 'just like that', nothing ever was.

She'd better hurry up. Her front door remained determinedly closed. It was made of cheap varnished wood, with a mock-Georgian fanlight, and was the spit of every other door on the estate in Cherry Hinton. Jackson could have kicked it in without breaking a sweat. She was late. Her flight was at one and she should have been on her way to the airport by now. Jackson cracked the car window to let in some air and let out some smoke. She was always late.

Coffee was no good for punctuating the tedium, unless he was prepared to piss into a bottle, which he wasn't. Now that he was divorced he was free to use words like 'piss' and 'shit' – elements of his vocabulary almost eliminated by Josie. She was a primary-school teacher and spent much of her working day modifying the behaviour of five-year-old boys. When they were married she would come home and do the same to Jackson ('For God's sake, Jackson, use the proper word, it's a *penis*') during their evenings together, cooking pasta and yawning their way through crap on television. She wanted their daughter, Marlee, to grow up 'using the correct anatomical language for genitalia'. Jackson would rather Marlee grew up without knowing genitalia even existed, let alone informing him that she had been 'made' when he 'put his penis in Mummy's vagina', an oddly clinical description for an urgent, sweatily precipitate event that had taken place in a field somewhere off the A1066 between Thetford and Diss, an acrobatic coupling in his old F Reg BMW (320i, two-door, definitely a policeman's car, much missed, RIP). That was in the days when a sudden desperate need to have sex was commonplace between them and the only thing that had made this particular incidence memorable had been Josie's uncharacteristically Russian-roulette attitude to birth control.

Later she blamed the consequence (Marlee) on his own unpreparedness but Jackson thought Marlee was a winning result, and anyway what did Josie expect if she started fondling his – and let's be anatomically correct here – penis while all he was trying to do was get to Diss, although for what reason was now lost to time. Jackson himself was conceived during the course of a guest-house holiday in Ayrshire, a fact that his father had always found inexplicably amusing.

He shouldn't have thought about coffee because now there was a dull ache in his bladder. When *Woman's Hour* finished he put Allison Moorer's *Alabama Song* on the CD player, an album which he found comfortingly melancholic. *Bonjour Tristesse*. Jackson was going to French classes with a view to the day when he could sell up and move abroad and do whatever people did when they retired early. Golf? Did the French play golf? Jackson couldn't think of the names of any French golfers so that was a good sign because Jackson hated golf. Maybe he could just play boules and smoke himself to death. The French were good at smoking.

Jackson had never felt at home in Cambridge, never felt at home in the south of England if it came to that. He had come here more or less by accident, following a girlfriend and staying for a wife. For years he had thought about moving back north, but he knew he never would. There was nothing there for him, just bad memories and a past he could never undo, and what was the point anyway when France was laid out on the other side of the Channel like an exotic patchwork of sunflowers and grapevines and little cafés where he could sit all afternoon drinking local wine and bitter espressos and smoking Gitanes, where everyone would say, *Bonjour, Jackson*, except they would pronounce it 'zhaksong', and he would be happy. Which was exactly the opposite of how he felt now.

Of course, at the rate he was going it wouldn't be early retirement, just retirement. Jackson could remember when he was a kid and retired men were the old guys who tottered between the allotment and the corner of the snug. They had seemed like *really* old guys but maybe they weren't much older than he was now. Jackson was forty-five but felt much,

much older. He was at that dangerous age when men suddenly notice that they're going to die eventually, inevitably, and there isn't a damn thing they can do about it, but that doesn't stop them trying, whether it's shagging anything that moves or listening to early Bruce Springsteen and buying a top-of-the-range motorbike (a BMW K 1200 LT usually, thus considerably upping their chances of meeting death even earlier than anticipated). Then there were the guys who found themselves in the rut of routine alcoholic tedium – the lost and lonesome highway of your average beta male (his father's way). And then there was Jackson's own chosen path that led to the everyday Zen of a French house with its white stucco walls, geraniums in pots on the windowsills, a blue door, the paint peeling because who gives a damn about house maintenance in rural France?

He had parked in the shade but the sun had moved higher in the sky now and the temperature in the car was becoming uncomfortable. She was called Nicola Spencer and she was twenty-nine years old and lived in a neat ghetto of brick-built houses. The houses and the streets all looked the same to Jackson and if he lost his bearings for a moment he ended up in a Bermuda triangle of identical open-plan front lawns. Jackson had an almost unreasonable prejudice against housing estates. This prejudice was not unrelated to his ex-wife and his ex-marriage. It was Josie who had wanted a house on a new estate, Josie who had been one of the first people to sign up to live in Cambourne, the purpose-built Disney-like 'community' outside Cambridge with its cricket pitch on the 'traditional' village green, its 'Roman-themed play area'. It was Josie who had moved them into the house when the street was still a building site and insisted that they furnish it with practical modern designs, who had rejected Victoriana as cluttered, who had thought an excess of carpets and curtains was 'suffocating' and yet now she was inhabiting ye olde curiosity shop with David Lastingham – a Victorian terrace crammed with antique furniture that he'd inherited from his parents, every available surface swathed and draped and curtained. ('You're sure he's not gay then?' Jackson had asked Josie, just to rile her – the guy had professional manicures, for heaven's sake – and she'd laughed and said, 'He's not insecure with his masculinity, Jackson.')

Jackson could feel the ache in his jaw starting up again. He was currently seeing more of his dentist than he had of his wife in the last year of their marriage. His dentist was called Sharon and was what his father used to refer to as 'stacked'. She was thirty-six and drove a BMW Z3, which was a bit of a hairdresser's car in Jackson's opinion, but nonetheless he found her very attractive. Unfortunately, there was no possibility of having a relationship with someone who had to put on a mask, protective glasses and gloves to touch you. (Or one who peered into your mouth and murmured, 'Smoking, Jackson?')

He opened an out-of-date copy of *Le Nouvel Observateur* and tried to read it because his French teacher said they should immerse themselves in French culture, even if they didn't understand it. Jackson could only pick out the odd word that meant anything and he could see subjunctives scatter-gunned all over the place – if ever there was an unnecessary tense it was the French subjunctive. His eyes drifted drowsily over the page. A lot of his life these days consisted of simply waiting, something he would have been useless at twenty years ago but which he now found almost agreeable. Doing nothing was much more productive than people thought. Jackson often had his most profound insights when he appeared to be entirely idle. He didn't get bored, he just went into a nothing kind of place. He thought sometimes he would like to enter a monastery, that he would be good at being an ascetic, an anchorite, a Zen monk.

Jackson had arrested a jeweller once, an old guy who'd been fencing stolen property, and when Jackson came looking for him in his workshop he'd found him sitting in an ancient armchair, smoking his pipe and contemplating a piece of rock on his workbench. Without saying anything, he took the rock and placed it in Jackson's palm, as if it was a gift. Jackson was reminded of his biology teacher from school, who would hand you something – a bird's egg, a leaf – and make you explain it to him rather than the other way round. The rock was a dark ironstone that looked like petrified tree-bark and sandwiched in the centre of it was a seam of milky opal, like a hazy summer sky at dawn. A notoriously tricky stone to work, the old man informed Jackson. He had been looking at it for two weeks now, he said, another two weeks and he might be ready to start cutting it and Jackson said that in another two weeks he would be in a remand prison some-where, but the guy had a great lawyer and made bail and got away with a suspended sentence.

A year later Jackson received a parcel addressed to him at the police station. Inside there was no note, just a box, and in a nest lined with midnight-blue velvet was an opal pendant, a little plaque of sky. Jackson knew he was being given a lesson by the old man, but it had taken him many years to understand it. He was keeping the pendant for Marlee's eighteenth birthday.

Nicola's husband, Steve Spencer, was convinced his wife 'had taken a lover' – that's how he put it, so it sounded delicate and rather courtly to Jackson's ears, whereas most of the suspicious spouses who came to him tended to voice their mistrust in cruder terms. Steve was the nervy, paranoid type and he couldn't understand how he'd managed to net someone like Nicola, because she was 'so gorgeous'. Jackson had known gorgeous in his time and it wasn't the Nicola Spencers of the world, although he thought that if he was married to Steve Spencer he might be tempted to 'take a lover'. Steve was a pharmacist in a chain of chemists and seemed to have no hobbies or interests other than Nicola. She was 'the only woman in the world' for him. Jackson had never believed that there was one person in the world that you were destined for. And if there was, knowing his luck, she'd be working in a rice field in the middle of China or be a convicted killer on the run.

When she wasn't at work, Nicola Spencer went to the gym, to Sainsbury's (and once, for no apparent reason, to Tesco's), her mother's, a friend called Louise and a friend called

Vanessa. Vanessa was part of a married couple – Vanessa and Mike – who were also friends of 'Steve and Nicola'. Louise and Vanessa, as far as Jackson could tell, didn't know each other. Nicola also went regularly to the garage, for petrol obviously, and in the garage shop she sometimes bought milk and nearly always bought chocolate and a copy of *Hello!* or *Heat.* She had also been to a garden centre, where she bought a tray of bedding plants which she put straight into the garden and then failed to water, judging by the look of them when Jackson climbed up on the garden fence to have a snoop at what went on chez Spencer, or, more accurately, *au jardin* Spencer.

In the last four weeks Nicola had also been to a DIY superstore where she bought a screwdriver and a Stanley knife, to Habitat where she bought a table lamp, to Top Shop for a white T-shirt, Next for a white blouse, to Boots (twice for cosmetics and toiletries and once with a prescription for Ponstan), Robert Sayle's for two blue hand towels, and to a fish stall on the market where she bought (expensive) monk-fish for a meal, for the aforesaid Vanessa and Mike, which Steve Spencer later reported to have been 'a disaster'. Nicola was not a great cook apparently. She also led a bloody boring life, unless something fantastically interesting happened to her when she was pushing a trolley up and down the economy aisles of her airline. Is that what had happened to Josie when she 'took' David Lastingham, was she just so bored with Jackson that she couldn't bear it any more? She met him at a party, a party that Jackson hadn't gone to because he was working, and the pair of them had 'tried to control their feelings' but they obviously hadn't tried hard enough because within six months they were taking each other at every available clandestine opportunity and now David Lastingham got to put his penis in Mummy's vagina whenever he felt like it.

Josie had filed for divorce as soon as it was possible. Irretrievable breakdown – as if it was all his fault and she wasn't shagging some poncy guy with a goatee. ('David,' Marlee said, not as grudgingly as Jackson would have liked.

'He's all right, he buys me chocolate, he makes nice pasta.' It was a six-lane motorway from that girl's stomach to her heart. 'I cook nice pasta,' Jackson said and heard how childish that sounded and didn't care. Jackson had got someone he knew to look up David Lastingham on the paedophile register. Just in case.)

Jackson smoked the last cigarette. Nicola hadn't done anything the least suspicious on Jackson's watch so if she was having an affair then she must be literally playing away from home – all those stopovers in mid-range hotels, warm evenings and cheap alcohol provided the perfect conditions for fostering bad behaviour. Jackson had tried to explain to Steve that he was going to have to pay for Jackson to fly with Nicola if he really wanted to find out if anything was going on but Steve wasn't keen to fund what he seemed to think would be a free holiday abroad for Jackson. Jackson thought he might just go anyway and then do some creative accounting when it came to the bill, a return trip to almost anywhere in Europe could easily disappear into the catch-all heading of 'Sundries'. Maybe he would wait until she was on a flight to France and tag along. Jackson didn't want a holiday, he wanted a new life. And he wanted to be finished with Nicola Spencer and her own dull life.

When Jackson had set up as a private investigator two years ago he had no expectation of it being a glamorous profession. He'd already been a member of the Cambridgeshire Constabulary for twelve years and before that he was in the military police, so he had no illusions about the ways of the world. Investigating other people's tragedies and cock-ups and misfortunes was all he knew. He was used to being a voyeur, the outsider looking in, and nothing, but nothing, that anyone did surprised him any more. Yet despite everything he'd seen and done, inside Jackson there remained a belief – a small, battered and bruised belief – that his job was to help people be good rather than punish them for being bad.

He left the police and set up the investigation agency after his marriage disappeared in front of his eyes. 'What about your pension?' Josie said to him. 'What about it?' Jackson said, a cavalier attitude he was beginning to regret.

For the most part, the work he undertook now was either irksome or dull – process-serving, background-checking and bad debts and hunting down the odd rogue tradesman that the police would never get round to ('I gave him £300 up front for materials and I never saw him again.' Surprise, surprise.) Not to forget missing cats.

On cue, Jackson's mobile rang, a tinny rendition of *Carmina Burana*, a ringtone reserved exclusively for Binky Rain ('Binky' – what kind of a name *was* that? Really?). Binky Rain was the first client Jackson had acquired when he set up as a private investigator and he supposed he would never be rid of her until he retired and even then he could imagine her following him to France, a string of stray cats behind her, Pied Piper-like. She was a catwoman, the mad, old bat variety that kept an open door for every feline slacker in Cambridge.

Binky was over ninety and was the widow of 'a Peterhouse fellow', a philosophy don (despite living in Cambridge for fourteen years, Jackson still thought of the mafia when he heard that word). 'Dr Rain' – Julian – had long gone to rest in the great Senior Common Room in the sky. Binky herself had been brought up in colonial Africa and treated Jackson like a servant, which was how she treated everyone. She lived in Newnham, on the way to Grantchester Meadows, in a bungalow which must once have been a perfectly normal between-the-wars redbrick but which years of neglect had transformed into an overgrown gothic horror. The place was crawling with cats, hundreds of the damn things. Jackson got the heebie-jeebies just thinking about the smell – cat urine, tom-cat spray, saucers of tinned food on every surface, the cheap stuff that was made from the parts of animals that even the burger chains shunned. Binky Rain had no money, no friends and no family and her neighbours avoided her and yet she effortlessly maintained the façade of aristocratic hauteur, like a refugee from some ancien régime, living out her life in tatters. Binky Rain was exactly the kind of person whose body lay undiscovered in their house for weeks, except that her cats would probably have eaten her by the time she was found.

Her complaint, the reason she had originally engaged Jackson's services, was that someone was stealing her cats. Jackson couldn't work out whether cats really did go missing or whether she just thought they went missing. She had this thing about black cats in particular. 'Someone's taking them,' she said in her clipped little voice, her accent as anachronistic as everything else about her, a remnant, a leftover from another time, another place, long turned into history. The first cat to go missing was a black cat ('bleck ket') called Nigger – and Binky Rain thought that was all right! Not named after a black man ('bleck men'), she said dismissively when his jaw dropped, but after Captain Scott's cat on the *Discovery*. (Did she really go around the quiet streets of Newnham, shouting, 'Nigger!'? Dear God, please not.) Her brother-in-law had been a stalwart of the Scott Polar Research Institute on Lensfield Road and had spent a winter camped on the ice of the Ross Shelf, thus making Binky an expert on Antarctic exploration, apparently. Scott was 'a fool', Shackleton 'a womanizer' and Peary 'an American', which seemed to be enough of a condemnation in itself. The way Binky talked about polar expeditions ('Horses! Only an idiot would take horses!') belied the fact that the most challenging journey she had undertaken was the voyage from Cape Town to Southampton in first class on the *Dunnottar Castle* in 1938.

Jackson's best friend, Howell, was black and when Jackson told him about Binky having a cat called Nigger he roared with laughter. Howell dated from Jackson's army days, when they had started out as squaddies together. '"Bleck men",' Howell laughed, doing a disturbing impression of an old white lady, disturbing given that Howell was six foot six and the blackest black man Jackson had ever met. After his discharge, Howell had returned to his native Birmingham and was currently working as a doorman for a large hotel, a job that required him to wear a ridiculous pantomime costume – a royal-blue frock coat covered in gold braid and, even more ridiculously, a top hat. Howell had such an imposing presence that rather than losing dignity in this flunky's outfit he actually made it seem strangely distinguished.

Howell must be at a dangerous age as well. What was he doing about it? It must be over six months since they had spoken. That was how you lost people, a little carelessness and they just slipped through your fingers. Jackson missed Howell. Somewhere along the line Jackson had managed to lose not only his wife and child but all of his friends as well. (Although had he had any friends other than Howell?) Maybe this was why people filled their house with stinking cats, so they didn't notice that they were alone, so they wouldn't die without a living soul noticing. Jackson hoped that wouldn't happen to him. Anyway, he was going to die in France, in a chair, in the garden, after a good meal. Perhaps Marlee would be there on a visit, and she would have her children with her so that Jackson could see that part of him carried on into the future, that death wasn't the end of everything.

Jackson let his voicemail pick up Binky's message and then listened back to her imperial tones commanding him to visit her as soon as possible on 'a matter of some urgency' to do with 'Frisky'.

Binky Rain had never paid Jackson in the two years he had known her but he supposed this was fair as, for his part, he had never found a single missing cat in those two years. He saw his visits to her more as a social service. No one else ever visited the poor old cow and Jackson had a tolerance for her idiosyncrasies that surprised even himself. She was an old Nazi boot but you had to admire her spirit. Why did she think people were taking her cats? Jackson thought it would be vivisection – the usual paranoid belief of cat lovers – but no, according to Binky they took them to make gloves out of them. (Bleck gloves, obviously.)

Jackson was just debating with himself whether to give up on tardy Nicola and obey Binky's summons when the front door flew open. Jackson slid down in the driver's seat and pretended to be concentrating on *Le Nouvel Observateur*. He could see from fifty yards away that Nicola was in a bad mood, although that was more or less her default setting. She looked hot, already tightly buttoned into the airline's ugly uniform. The uniform didn't show off her figure and the courts she was wearing – like the Queen's shoes – made her ankles look thick. When she was running was the only time Jackson saw Nicola without make-up. *Au naturel*. She ran like someone training for a marathon. Jackson was a runner – he ran three miles every morning, up at six, out on the street, back for coffee, before most people were up. That was what army training did for you. Army, the police and a hefty dose of Scottish Presbyterian genes. ('Always running, Jackson,' Josie said. 'If you run for ever you come back to where you started from – that's the curvature of space for you, did you know that?')

Nicola looked much better in her running clothes. In her uniform she looked frumpy, but when she ran around the maze of streets where she lived she looked athletic and strong. For running, she wore tracksuit bottoms and an old Blue Jays T-shirt she must have picked up in Toronto although she hadn't flown across the Atlantic during the time that Jackson had been watching her. She had been to Milan three times, Rome twice, and once each to Madrid, Düsseldorf, Perpignan, Naples and Faro.

Nicola got in her car, a little girly Ford Ka, and took off like a rocket for Stansted. Jackson wasn't exactly a slow driver but Nicola went at terrifying speeds. When this was over he was considering alerting someone in traffic. Jackson had done a stint in traffic before plainclothes and there were times when he would have liked to pull Nicola over and arrest her.

His phone rang again as the traffic slowed in a holding pattern around Stansted. This time it was his secretary, Deborah, who snapped, 'Where are you?' as if he was supposed to be somewhere else.

'I'm fine, thank you, how are you?'

'Someone phoned, you may as well go and see them while you're out and about.' Deborah said 'out and about' as if Jackson was getting drunk or picking up women.

'Do you want to enlighten me further?' he asked.

'No,' Deborah said. 'Something about finding something.'

*

Once Nicola arrived at the airport her movements followed their usual routine. She parked her car and went inside the terminal. Jackson watched her until she disappeared from view. After that he went to the toilets, had a double espresso that did nothing to cool down the heat of the day, purchased cigarettes, read the headlines in a newspaper that he didn't buy and then drove away again.

By the time Nicola's plane to Prague was climbing steeply away from the flat countryside below, Jackson was walking up the path of a large house on Owlstone Road, frighteningly close to where Binky Rain lived. The door was answered by a woman stranded somewhere in her forties who squinted at Jackson over the top of a pair of half-moon spectacles. Academic, he thought to himself.

'Mrs Land?' Jackson said.

'Miss Land,' she said, 'Amelia Land. Thank you for coming.'

Amelia Land made a terrible cup of coffee. Jackson could already feel its corrosive effect on his stomach. She was wandering around the neglected kitchen, searching for biscuits, even though Jackson had told her twice that he didn't want one, thank you. Finally, she retrieved a packet of damp digestives from the depths of a cupboard and Jackson ate one just to keep her happy. The biscuit was like soft, stale sand in his mouth, but Amelia Land seemed satisfied that her duty as a hostess had been done.

She seemed very distracted, even mildly deranged, but, living in Cambridge, Jackson had got used to university types, although she said she lived in 'Oxford, not Cambridge, it's a *completely* different place', and Jackson had thought, yeah, right, but said nothing. Amelia Land kept babbling on about blue mice and when he'd said gently to her, 'Start at the beginning, Miss Land,' she'd carried on with the blue-mice theme and said that *was* the beginning, and, 'Please call me Amelia.' Jackson sighed inwardly, sensing this tale was going to take a lot of coaxing.

The sister appeared, disappeared and then reappeared, holding in her hand what looked like an old doll. You would never have taken them for sisters, one tall and heavy, her hair greying and falling out of a kind of topknot, the other short and curvy and – Jackson knew this type too – flirting with anything male and still breathing. The short one wore bright-red lipstick and was dressed in what looked like second-hand clothes, layers of mismatched eccentric garments, her wild hair piled haphazardly on her head and fixed with a pencil. They were both dressed for cold weather rather than the sweltering day outside. Jackson could see why – he had shivered as he crossed the threshold, leaving the sunshine behind for the wintry gloom of the interior.

'Our father died two days ago,' Julia said, as if it was an everyday nuisance. Jackson looked at the doll on the table. It was made of some kind of grubby towelling material and had long thin legs and arms and the head of a mouse. And it was blue. Understanding finally dawned. He nodded at it. 'A blue mouse,' he said to Amelia.

'No, *the* Blue Mouse,' she said, as if that distinction was vital. Amelia Land might as well have had 'unloved' tattooed on her forehead. She was dressed in a way that suggested she'd stopped shopping for new clothes twenty years ago and that when she had shopped for clothes it had been exclusively in Laura Ashley. The way she was dressed reminded him of old photographs of fishwives – clumpy shoes and woollen tights and a cord dirndl skirt and around her shoulders some kind of shawl that she was hugging to herself as if she was freezing, which wasn't a surprise because this place was *Baltic*, Jackson thought. It was as if the house had its own climate.

'Our father died,' Amelia said brusquely, 'two days ago.'

'Yes,' Jackson said carefully, 'your sister just said that. I'm sorry for your loss,' he added, rather perfunctorily because he could see that neither of them seemed particularly sorry.

Amelia frowned and said, 'What I mean is . . .' She looked at her sister for help. That was the trouble with academic types, Jackson thought, never able to say what they mean and half the time never meaning what they say.

'Let me hazard a guess,' he said helpfully. 'Your father died . . .' They both nodded vigorously as if relieved that Jackson had grasped this point. 'Your father died,' he continued, 'and you started clearing out the old family home . . .' He hesitated because they looked less sure of this. 'This *is* the old family home?'

'Well, yes,' Julia said. 'It's just –' she shrugged – 'that sounds so *warm*, you know. "Old family home".'

'Well,' Jackson said, 'how about we remove any emotional significance from those three words and just treat them as two adjectives and a noun. Old. Family. Home. True or false?'

'True,' Julia admitted reluctantly.

'Of course, strictly speaking,' Amelia said, staring out of the kitchen window as if she was talking to someone in the garden, '"family" isn't an adjective. "Familial" would be the adjective.'

Jackson decided the best thing would be to carry on as if she hadn't spoken. 'Not close to the old guy then?' he said, to Julia.

'No, we weren't,' Amelia said, turning round and giving him her full attention. 'And we found this in a locked drawer in his study.' The blue mouse again. The Blue Mouse.

'And the significance of the "Blue Mouse"?' Jackson prompted. He hoped they hadn't just discovered their old man was some kind of soft-toy fetishist.

'Did you ever hear of Olivia Land?' Julia asked.

'Rings a bell,' Jackson said. A very small bell. 'A relative?'

'She was our sister,' Amelia said. 'She disappeared thirty-four years ago. She was taken.'

Taken? Oh, not alien abduction, that would really make his day. Julia took out a packet of cigarettes and offered him one. She made offering a cigarette seem like an invitation to sex. He could feel the sister's disapproval from where he sat, but whether it was of the nicotine or the sex he wasn't sure. Both probably. He declined the cigarette – he would never have smoked in front of a client anyway – but he inhaled deeply when Julia lit up.

'She was kidnapped,' Julia said, 'from a tent in the garden.'

'A tent?'

'It was summer,' Amelia said sharply. 'Children sleep outside in tents in the summer.'

'So they do,' Jackson said mildly. Somehow he had the feeling that Amelia Land had been the one in the tent with the sister.

'She was only three,' Julia said. 'She was never found.'

'You really don't know the case?' Amelia said. 'It was very big.'

'I'm not from this area,' Jackson said, and thought of all the girls who must have disappeared over the last thirty-four years. But, of course, as far as the Land sisters were concerned there was only one. He felt suddenly too sad and too old.

'It was very hot,' Amelia said, 'a heat wave.'

'Like now?'

'Yes. Aren't you going to take notes?'

'Would it make you happier if I did?' he asked.

'No,' Amelia snapped.

They had obviously reached some kind of conversational impasse. Jackson looked at the Blue Mouse. It had 'clue' written all over it. Jackson attempted to join the dots. 'So, let's see,' he ventured. 'This is Olivia's and she had it with her when she was abducted? And the first time it's been seen since is when it turns up after your father's death? And you didn't call the police?'

They both frowned. It was funny because although they looked quite different they shared exactly the same facial expressions. Jackson supposed that was what was meant by 'fleeting resemblance'.

'What wonderful powers of deduction you have, Mr Brodie,' Julia said and it was hard to tell whether she was being ironic or trying to flatter him. She had one of those husky voices that sounded as if she was permanently coming down with a cold. Men seemed to find that sexy in a woman, which Jackson thought was odd because it made women sound less like women and more like men. Maybe it was a gay thing.

'The police didn't find her *then*,' Amelia said, ignoring Julia, 'and they're not going to be interested *now*. And, anyway, maybe it's not a matter for the police.'

'But it's a matter for me?'

'Mr Brodie,' Julia said, very sweetly, too sweetly. They were like good cop, bad cop. 'Mr Brodie, we just want to know why Victor had Olivia's Blue Mouse.'

'Victor?'

'Daddy. It just seems . . .'

'Wrong?' Jackson supplied.

Jackson rented a house now, a long way from the Cambourne ghetto. It was a cottage really, in a row of similar small cottages, on a road that must once have been in the countryside. Farm cottages, probably. Whatever farm they had been a part of had long since been built over by streets of Victorian working-class terraces. Nowadays even back-to-backs with their front doors opening straight on to the street went for a fortune in the area. The poor moved out to the likes of Milton and Cherry Hinton but now even the council estates there had been colonized by middle-class university types (and the Nicola Spencers of the world), which must really piss the poor people off. The poor might always be with us but Jackson was puzzled as to where they actually lived these days.

When Josie left for non-connubial bliss with David Lastingham, Jackson considered staying on and living in the marital Lego house. This thought had occupied him for roughly ten minutes before he rang the estate agent and put it on the market. After they had split the proceeds of the sale there wasn't enough money left for Jackson to buy a new place, so he had chosen to rent this house instead. It was the last in the terrace, on the run-down side, and the walls between it and the house next door were so thin that you could hear every fart and cat mewl from the neighbours. The furnishings that came with it were cheap and it had an impersonal atmosphere, like a disappointing holiday home, that Jackson found strangely restful.

When he moved out of the house he had shared with his

wife and daughter, Jackson went round every room to check that nothing had been left behind, apart from their lives, of course. When he walked into the bathroom he realized that he could still smell Josie's perfume – L'Air du Temps – a scent she had worn long before he had ever met her. Now she wore the Joy by Patou that David Lastingham bought her, a scent so old-fashioned that it made her seem like a different woman, which she was, of course. The Josie he had known had rejected all the wifely attributes of her mother's generation. She was a lousy cook and didn't even possess a sewing basket but she did all the DIY in their little box house. She said to him once that when women learned that rawlplugs weren't the mysterious objects they thought they were, they would rule the world. Jackson had been under the impression they already did and made the mistake of voicing this opinion, which resulted in a statistical lecture about global gender politics – 'Two thirds of the world's work done by women, Jackson, yet they only own one tenth of the world's property – do you see any problem with that?' (Yes, he did.) Now, of course, she had turned into retro-woman, a kind of Stepford wife, who baked bread and was going to knitting classes. Knitting! What kind of a joke was that?

When he moved into the rented house he bought a bottle of L'Air du Temps and sprayed the tiny bathroom with it, but it wasn't the same.

Amelia and Julia had given him a photograph, a small, square faded colour photograph from another time. It was a close-up of Olivia, grinning for the camera, all her regular little teeth on show. There were freckles on her snub nose and her hair was looped up in short plaits, tied with green and white gingham ribbons although all the colours in the photograph had acquired a yellow tint with age. She was wearing a dress that matched the ribbons, the smocking on the dress partly concealed by the blue mouse which she was clutching to her chest. Jackson could tell she was making the blue mouse pose for the camera, he could almost hear her telling it to smile, but its features, appliquéd in black wool, carried the same air of gravity then that they did now, except that time had robbed the blue mouse of half an eye and a nostril.

It was the same photograph that the papers had used. Jackson had looked up the microfiche files on his way home. There were pages and pages about the search for Olivia Land, the story ran for weeks, and Amelia was right – the big story before Olivia had been the heat wave. Jackson tried to remember thirty-four years ago. He would have been eleven years old. Had it been hot? He had no idea. He couldn't remember eleven. The important thing about it was that it wasn't twelve. All the years before he was twelve shone with an unblemished and immaculate light. After twelve it was dark.

He listened to the messages on his answering machine. One from his daughter, Marlee, complaining that her mother wouldn't let her go to an open-air concert on Parker's Piece and would Jackson talk to her, please, please? (Marlee was eight, no way was she going to an open-air concert); another 'Frisky' message from Binky Rain and one from his secretary, Deborah Arnold, berating him for not coming back into the office. She was ringing from home, he could hear two of her loutish teenagers talking in the background over the blare of MTV. Deborah had to shout in order to inform him that there was 'a Theo Wyre' trying to get in touch with him and she didn't know what it was about except that he 'seemed to have lost something'. The name 'Theo Wyre' sounded startlingly familiar but he couldn't place it. Old age, he supposed.

Jackson fetched a Tiger beer from the fridge, pulled off his boots (Magnum Stealths, the only boot as far as Jackson was concerned), lay down on the uncomfortable couch and reached over to his CD player (the good thing about living in a tiny house was that he could touch almost everything in the room without getting up) and put on Trisha Yearwood's 1995 *Thinkin' About You* album, now deleted for some reason. Trisha might be mainstream, but that didn't mean she wasn't good. She understood pain. He opened *An Introduction to French Grammar* and tried to focus on the correct formation of the past tense using *être* (although when

41

he lived in France there would be no past and no future, only present) but it was difficult to concentrate because the gum above his rogue tooth was throbbing.

Jackson sighed and retrieved the blue mouse from the mantelpiece and placed it against his shoulder and patted its small, soft back, in much the same way he had once comforted Marlee when she was small. The blue mouse felt cold, as if it had been in a dark place for a long time. Not for a moment did Jackson think that he could find that little girl with the gingham ribbons in her plaits.

Jackson closed his eyes and opened them again immediately because he'd suddenly remembered who Theo Wyre was. Jackson groaned. He didn't want to remember Theo Wyre. He didn't want anything to do with Theo Wyre.

Trisha was singing 'On a Bus to St Cloud'. Sometimes it seemed to him as if the entire world consisted of the one accounting sheet – lost on the left-hand side, found on the right. Unfortunately the two never balanced. Amelia and Julia Land had found something, Theo Wyre had lost something. How easy life would be if it could be one and the same thing.

GOODBYE AGAIN

BY WILLIAM COOK

The cheerfully dissipated Peter Cook and his diminutive chum
Dudley Moore first worked together as half of the *Beyond the
Fringe* team, with Alan Bennett and Jonathan Miller. Their
best work was performed together, and although most of the
ideas were Cook's, there is no question that Dudley was more
than just a straight man. *Goodbye Again* is an unmissable
collection, which represents the whole of their hilarious
oeuvre.

The first few chapters collect the scripts from their stage
and television shows, including the superb 'Dagenham
Dialogues', in which the pair would sit with their caps and
pints, discussing everything from ants to Hollywood. At their
best these deadpan musings achieved a brilliantly surreal
quality. Ill-tempered gems such as 'The Most Boring Man in
the World Competition' are reproduced in full, and it's
impossible to read these classic conversations without
picturing Peter's mischievous delight as Dudley chokes with
suppressed giggles.

One of the hallmarks of their act was mutual amusement, a
sense that the audience was eavesdropping rather than being
'performed at', and their work reflects their complex personal
and professional partnership. When this was soured by
Dudley's Hollywood success and Peter's intemperate drinking
habits, the wanton malice and transcendent vulgarity of the
infamous Derek and Clive routines reflected this bitterness
and misanthropy.

This comprehensive comedic collection is essential reading

for the young, the old, (and the shamelessly immature); indeed anyone who still wriggles with guilty mirth at such unedifying classics as 'Winky Wanky Woo'. Theirs was perfect comic writing. Without these apparently artless, but sublimely funny sketches, Monty Python, the Comic Strip, Blackadder, and nearly all subsequent British comedy would be infinitely poorer.

A volume of Peter's letters, journalism and solo sketches is also in print, entitled 'Tragically I Was an Only Twin', which includes the peculiar thoughts of E. L. Wisty, scurrilous *Private Eye* contributions and his enthusiastic, unorthodox sports writing.

Recommended by Mike Woods,
www.waterstones.co.uk

£17.99
ISBN: 1844134008
Published October 2004

THE GLIDD OF GLOOD

(BBC2, 1970)

Peter was always swift to acknowledge his debt to the doyens of Victorian nonsense verse, Edward Lear and Lewis Carroll. In the first series of Not Only But Also, *Peter and Dudley dramatised one of Lear's poems, 'Incidents in the Life of my Uncle Arly', with Peter playing Uncle Arly. In the second series, they filmed Carroll's 'The Walrus And The Carpenter' from* Alice's Adventures in Wonderland. *Dudley played the Walrus and Peter played the Carpenter, in a minimalist rendition that anticipated Jonathan Miller's bold BBC adaptation of the novel (with Peter as the Mad Hatter) later that year. There are dashes of Lear and Carroll in much of Peter's solo work, especially his early monologues, but no other sketch pays more direct homage to that genre than this mock heroic poem – a 'Jabberwocky' style doggerel which bears comparison with 'The Owl And The Pussycat', or anything in* Through The Looking Glass.

'The Glidd of Glood' was borrowed from Peter's never-to-be-finished book of children's verse – and if this remnant is anything to go by, it's a great shame it remained incomplete. The influence of Carroll is impossible to ignore, but it's still an original and idiosyncratic piece, which made a striking piece of film – not laugh-out-loud funny, but riveting nonetheless. Peter played the Glidd of Glood, dressed only in brown paper, plied with brandy by producer Jimmy Gilbert to keep out the winter cold. Dudley played Sparquin, the court jester, and the suitably bleak setting was Bodiam Castle – a windswept ruin on the south coast.

The Glidd of Glood would wander nude throughout his
spacious castle
So everyone could plainly see his huge brown paper parcel

In this the Glidd kept carefully hid his jewels, gold and crown,
Tied to his wrists with bits of string – he never put it down

There's never been a man so mean – he didn't mind the cold
When clothes grow old their value goes – unlike a piece of
gold

And when the Glidd got into bed, he'd cuddle with his
treasure
And kissed his parcel constantly – this was his only pleasure

His servants all were quite appalled of everything he did
But no one dared to say a word – they feared the cruel Glidd

For he could kill a man at will – his power was absolute
And every night, at half past eight, they'd smile and kiss his
foot

'Oh Glidd of Glood, you are so good, as any Gloodite knows'
They whispered this each time they kissed his gnarled and
grimy toes

And when they ate it was their fate to sit with him at table
And look as grateful as they could – but very few were able

To save on food he fed them wood, mixed up with grains of
rice
On Sundays, as a special treat, he served them boiled mice

When in the mood, the Glidd of Glood would have a bit of fun
With Sparquin, the court jester, a man of eighty-one

Who'd say 'I say, I say, I say – who does not love our Glidd?
I beg you, stand and raise your hand' – but no one ever did

'We love him so because we know that nowhere could we find
A man so generous and true, so gentle and so kind

Oh lovely Glidd, we love you so – I kiss your knee, I suck your
toe
Oh lovely Glidd, don't ever go'

And then the Glidd would sternly bid them drink the moral
toast
With water from a plastic cup, one quarter full at most

The Glidd of Glood thought he saw God, one dark and
stormy night
A figure with a green moustache, and clad in shrouds of white

'You ghastly Glidd,' the vision said, 'Get on your knees and
pray,
If you want to enter paradise, you give all your wealth away'

'What? All of it?' replied the Glidd – 'my crown and jewels as
well?'
'Yes, all of it, you greedy twit – or else you'll burn in hell'

In wild despair, with many a tear, the Glidd undid the strings
And handed over jewels and crown, and all his precious
things

The sobbing Glidd returned to bed, to moan and weep and
fret
And when the sun came up at dawn, his sheets were soaking
wet

His morning tea arrived and he shrieked as he seized the cup
'Fetch me Sparquin here at once! I need some cheering up!'

'I fear he's gone,' replied the man – 'he caught the morning
flight,
He left behind this green moustache, and long white nighty

And here's a note that Sparquin wrote – it seems a little odd
It says 'Goodbye, you greedy Glidd,' signed Sparquin, alias
   God

The Glidd fell ill, a sudden chill, and very soon he died
The funeral was a gay affair, and not Gloodite cried

They drank and sang, the church bells rang, and then there
   was a dance
No flowers decked his grave save one, signed 'Sparquin, South
   of France'

And here's the moral of this tale of greed and gross deceit
If God asks you for all your cash, do ask for a receipt

SQUATTER AND THE ANT
(DEREK & CLIVE (LIVE), 1976)

This creepy sketch was a continuation of Peter's lifelong passion for creepy crawlies – a fascination that dated back to his boyhood in Torquay. Peter's early childhood coincided with the Second World War, and with most men away (his father included) the gardener was one of his few male role models. Poignantly, in a home movie, Peter can be seen following the gardener around the flower beds, imitating his spadework with his own tiny trowel. This may account for Peter's unusual fondness for insects (on the other hand, it may very well not), but either way, 'Squatter and the Ant' is far darker than most of his anthropomorphic fantasies. Again, this version contains material cut from the record, indicated by square brackets for hardcore fans.

(Peter and Dudley play a couple of upper-class old buffers.)

PETER: Have you heard anything recently of Squatter?

DUDLEY: No.

PETER: No, I wouldn't think you would have heard anything of Squatter.

DUDLEY: What's he up to at the moment?

PETER: Squatter Madras? Well, he tends to lie a bit low, you know.

DUDLEY: Really? Why's that?

PETER: Well, that's the way he lies – a bit low, which is the best way to lie, I think, in my view. But Squatter was one of my very best friends, which was him and, um, and him. He is in fact my only best friend. But Squatter had this incredible quality, which was, um, I don't know how you can define it, but I would say it was stupidity, which very few people I've known have got, to quite the same extent that Squatter has. I don't know if I've ever told you the story about Squatter and the ant.

DUDLEY: No, no, no.

PETER: Have I told you about Squatter and the ant?

DUDLEY: No, no, no.

PETER: Well, Squatter was in a terrible position. He was in Bahrain, which is a pretty bloody place to be, and there was this ant, which had only one leg.

DUDLEY: God.

PETER: And only one eye.

DUDLEY: God.

PETER: And was about two miles away from Squatter.

DUDLEY: God.

PETER: So, a pretty bloody menacing position for Squatter.

DUDLEY: Yes.

PETER: Who was equipped only with a hydrogen bomb.

DUDLEY: God.

PETER: Six grenades.

DUDLEY: God.

PETER: And a few rifles.

DUDLEY: Yes.

PETER: And this bloody ant, with one eye and one leg, was advancing towards Squatter, at say about a mile every century, you know.

DUDLEY: God.

PETER: Really speeding up. I think the animal was on drugs.

DUDLEY: Yes, or heat.

PETER: Or heat, yes, as you may say. And Squatter, with his extraordinary calm, took it very smoothly. And do you know what he did?

DUDLEY: No.

PETER: Nothing.

DUDLEY: Good God.

PETER: He immediately did nothing. And this stupefied the

ant. It stopped in its tracks. It didn't move an inch for about three and a half years. But still Squatter was very much aware of the problem of the ant, with all of one leg and all of one eye, advancing towards him. So he took up a strategic position – about five thousand men on one side, and seven thousand men on the other side, all equipped with various kinds of guns and so on. The ant was fairly pinpointed, but what was odd –

DUDLEY: Yes, go on – go on.

PETER: I will – was the ant understood Squatter. The ant realised he was up against somebody as good as he was.

DUDLEY: Some sort of understanding between them. They knew they were equals.

PETER: Equals in a struggle, yes. So Squatter, with a tremendous display of courage, put up his hands and surrendered. And the ant, five years laters –

DUDLEY: Five years laters?

PETER: Yes, five years laters – crept into the hole, and Squatter was gone. And this is the extraordinary thing about Squatter. He was never there when he was wanted. And Squatter told me later that he had gone because he'd had to go. That sums up Squatter for me.

DUDLEY: Yes, it's a sort of very simple approach to life.

PETER: The ant these days is writing its memoirs, you know, in the *Sunday Telegraph*, but Squatter . . .

DUDLEY: Squatter refuses to come out.

PETER: He refuses to comment on the whole situation. He just won't. He just won't. And I think he's quite right.

DUDLEY: I think he retains his dignity.

[PETER: He retains everying, including himself, which I think is only right.

DUDLEY: How is his arsehole these days?

PETER: Squatter's? Oh, why, it is in terrific form. Oh, he's got an enormous great party going on down there at the moment – Twiggy, Dustin Vulverne, John Prompt. Do you know John Prompt?

DUDLEY: Oh yes!

PETER: You do? I'm surprised. I never heard of him. John

Prompt is down there, and apparently he is making the whole party go with a tremendous swing. That's what a party needs to go with – a tremendous swing.]

DUDLEY: Yes. What I think is the tragedy about Squatter is that you know that one of these days . . .

PETER: Yes, one of these days.

DUDLEY: One of these days, he's going to let fly with the most enormous fart.

PETER: Well, this is the tragedy about Squatter. I mean, one has tried to hush it up. One has attempted to put cushions up his arse, one has attempted to do many things. But Squatter, taken unaware, may give fly to the most enormous fart, and this will be his undoing.

[DUDLEY: But not only his – also his arsehole's. I think there's going to be a frightful scene. You know, he has been eating solidly, let's face it, for sixty-four years, and without ever giving vent to his, er, things.

PETER: The necessary thing. He is, as the Spanish put it so quaintly, *constipado*.

DUDLEY: Yes, I think that's it.

PETER: *Un poco constipado.*

DUDLEY: *Conquisita pat chipata.*

PETER: Sixty-four years without ever letting forth a single . . .

DUDLEY: And the terrible thing is, one of these days he's going to crack – or his crack is going to.

PETER: One of these days, his crack is going to go, as you say.

DUDLEY: And there is going to be the most almighty Madras.

PETER: Well, this is Squatter's terrible problem.

DUDLEY: And you know, of course, what Madras is like. It is no fun at all!

PETER: It is no fun at all.

DUDLEY: Once that starts, or stuff, rather, starts coming out, it's going to burn his arsehole right off – it's going to take the lining off.

PETER: One thing I told Squatter about four years ago, I said, 'Squatter, if you allow yourself to be bunged up for another four years, you're going to go into orbit.' And Squatter turned to me, looked me straight in the eye, and he said, 'Fuck off.'

DUDLEY: Well, I pleaded with him. I said, 'Look, for God's sake,' I said. 'Let's have a look at your crack. For God's sake, let me line it with some Fairy, because otherwise it's going to be the most unholy mess.'

PETER: Or the most holy unmess.

DUDLEY: No, the most unholy mess. But he goes on and that's what –

PETER: But he doesn't go on. This is the problem. He never goes. He never goes on. He never starts. This is the trouble with Squatter. He has got, what, about sixty-five years of pent-up fury in his arsehole.

DUDLEY: Well, you know he is living in Blackpool now?

PETER: Well, it's a good place to –

DUDLEY: Very near the tower, and I was crossing the Atlantic –

PETER: Exploring North Sea Gas, I imagine.

DUDLEY: Air India, and I heard this faint rumbling and I knew it was from Blackpool and I thought, 'God! You know, it is not long, and that tower . . .'

PETER: Well, it's not long. It's reasonably long.

DUDLEY: That tower is going to be the first thing to go.

PETER: Yes, well, that's what I keep pleading with him.

DUDLEY: The whole of the British Isles is going to be covered with Madras. You know, with old Madras.

PETER: But how do you put this across? After all, he is an old friend.

DUDLEY: I don't know.

PETER: He is going to cover the world in a shower of shit.

DUDLEY: One has to tread very carefully here.

PETER: Yes, well, one will be unable to tread.

DUDLEY: Well, one will be. The situation will be out of one's hands. One will be presumably either floating or sinking, depending on the –

PETER: But what does one say to Squatter?

DUDLEY: On the texture of his expelling, expiring –

PETER: Build a hole and bung it in.]

DUDLEY: Well, I just wish him luck.

PETER: I wish him luck. At the same time, I wish him a strange sort of happiness – death.

DUDLEY: Yes, I think that would be the best thing for Squatter.

PETER: I think if death could come to Squatter now.

DUDLEY: Rather than the other way round.

PETER: Yes.

DUDLEY: I think we'd all be very happy.

PETER: I think so.

THE SCRIPTWRITER

(BBC2, 1970)

This was one of Dudley's favourite sketches (and one of producer Jimmy Gilbert's too) and although the idea of writers and producers haggling over swearwords may seem far-fetched, it's actually based on a real meeting, in which tits and bums were traded like percentage points in a showbiz contract. Even that grand old gent of Light Ent, Frank Muir, had endured such tussles with the BBC, and for entertainers like Peter and Dudley, the problem was even more pronounced. Peter and Dudley sidestepped the Corporation's self-censorship by adopting an ingenious ruse employed by hagglers throughout the ages. Instead of trimming their four-letter quotient in advance, they deliberately overloaded their work with bad language, so their subsequent concessions actually reduced the number of rude words to the requisite amount. *A similar ruse was used by Johnny Speight, who provided the inspiration for Dudley's part.*

For the benefit of younger readers, Speight's great sitcom, Till Death Us Do Part, *was about an East End bigot called Alf Garnett (immortalised by Warren Mitchell) whose racist rants were inevitably peppered with terms like 'bloody' and 'bugger'. Compared to the sort of phrases blokes like Garnett really use, Mitchell's language was actually quite restrained. Yet back then, the BBC was still in the business of teaching people how to speak, rather than reflecting how they really spoke – and despite the popularity of his creation, Speight had plenty of linguistic battles with the suits upstairs. 'You can't say "bloody" this many times,' they told him. 'You've already said "bum" five times.' 'All right,' said Speight. 'I'll drop one "bloody" if you'll let me have another "bum".' And it wasn't just the management who were squeamish about these Anglo Saxon idioms. When Gilbert's secretary typed up the script, she substituted 't*ts' for 'tits', proving that BBC executives weren't so out of touch with public opinion, after all. How times (and tastes) change. It all seems terribly mild by modern standards, and positively polite compared to Peter and Dudley's foul-mouthed alter egos, Derek & Clive.*

(Peter, Head of Light Entertainment, is in his office at the BBC. Enter a cockney scriptwriter called Johnny, aka Dudley)

PETER: My dear Johnny, come on in.

DUDLEY: Yes, I'd like a drink. Large Scotch and sherry, please.

PETER: Johnny, I want to tell you straight away, this is one of the funniest scripts I've ever read. It's witty, it's visual – but above all, it's damned funny.

DUDLEY: And it's got something to say. That's the point. It's got social comment about the bloody world we live in. Cheers!

PETER: This is what makes it so uniquely yours. Like all great comedy, it involved the audience. We want to do it, and, by

God, we will do it. It's terrific. Terrific.

DUDLEY: But?

PETER: But what, Johnny?

DUDLEY: You were about to say 'But . . .'

PETER: No, I wasn't. I think it's terrific, but . . .

DUDLEY: There you go.

PETER: Now, Johnny, you know perfectly well the BBC has been a pioneer in the field of controversial comedy – *TW3*, *Steptoe*, *Till Death* . . .

DUDLEY: What are you trying to say?

PETER: I'm just trying to say the BBC has led the way. You've got 27 bloodys in your script and I'm not worried.

DUDLEY: It reflects life, dunnit? I use bloody the whole bloody time.

PETER: Of course. Now the only thing that worries me about your script is the number of bums you have.

DUDLEY: What's the matter with that? I've got 31 bums in the script. They're all there for a dramatic, accumulative purpose. I mean, bums exist. You've got a bum.

PETER: I'm not trying to pretend that I don't have a bum, but what I do ask is whether a family audience wants to have a barrage of 31 bums fired into their living room at eight o'clock in the evening. My feeling – and I could be wrong – is that we're not ready to crash through the bum barrier yet.

DUDLEY: Yes, but only a year ago, Kenneth Tynan said . . .

PETER: I know perfectly well what Kenneth Tynan said, but that was a live, unscripted programme over which we had no control. I'm afraid we've never allowed a bum to get through until after eleven in the evening, and then only in a serious medical context.

DUDLEY: What miracle happens at 10.59 that suddenly takes the sting out of a bum?

PETER: I know it's illogical, Johnny. I'm willing to fight tooth and nail for your bums. We'll keep as many as possible. We'll have to lose a few. But there is one word in your script which you use several times that I'm even more worried about, and that's your colloquial word for a woman's chest.

DUDLEY: You mean my comedic use of the word tits?

PETER: Now that is a word you could use on a nature programme to describe the bird of the same name, or even in the phrase tit for tat, but not in the way you use it. Now Johnny, I think you'd lose none of the humour if you dropped them completely.

DUDLEY: They're a vital part of the vernacular. If I drop them, I wouldn't be true to myself as a writer. The whole point of the script would be lost if you snipped out the Bristols.

PETER: Now you've put your finger on it, Johnny. I think I could get a few bristols across without too much trouble.

DUDLEY: But bristols don't have the impact of tits.

PETER: You could use other rhyming slang, like sans or faintings.

DUDLEY: Sans or faintings? What are you talking about?

PETER: San Moritz. Fainting fits.

DUDLEY: That'll really get 'em going when this big bird goes by and the fella says, 'I wouldn't mind getting my sinkings round them faintings.'

PETER: Sinkings?

DUDLEY: Sinking sands – hands. Look, this isn't just a comedy – it's a social document. It mirrors the whole cosmic spectrum of our Zeitgeist.

PETER: Exactly. Your material is indestructible. You don't need to fall back on a bum or a thingummibob for a laugh.

DUDLEY: I'm not falling back on them. I'm using them as a comment. I mean you've got to have a go in life, haven't you? Those bums are more than just bums. They're used in a symbolic way. The bum represents the worker's struggle with his past.

PETER: Johnny, I realise how important these bums are to you.

DUDLEY: Not to mention the tits.

PETER: Yes, not to mention them. Now, as I respect you as a writer, I'm prepared to go out on a limb and allow you all of your 27 bloodys, let's say seven bums and, because it's you – I wouldn't do this for anybody else – as a special concession – and I'm really putting my head in the noose here – you can have one tit.

DUDLEY: Not even a pair?

PETER: Sorry, Johnny.

DUDLEY: Look, tell you what I'll do. I'll lose ten bloodys if you give me two more bums and an extra tit.

PETER: Right, that leaves you 17 bloodys, eight bums and a pair of doo das.

DUDLEY: Hold on. How many bloodys are there to a bum?

PETER: Let's say ten.

DUDLEY: Right, let's see. I can lose that one. Ten bloodys in the pub sequence – that gives me an extra bum to play with. But I think the scene in the launderette cries out for another tit.

PETER: So that's a deal. Seven bloodys, seven bums and three of the other.

DUDLEY: I raise you one bum.

PETER: You're really pushing me into a corner. But what's the point in letting one bum stand between us. Another bum it is. I'll whip the script off to Sooty this afternoon.

NELSON'S PURSE

BY MARTYN DOWNER

2005 sees the 200th anniversary of the Battle of Trafalgar. It is hardly surprising that a number of new books about Nelson are being published, but *Nelson's Purse* offers a new perspective.

In June 2002, Martyn Downer, then Head of Jewellery at Sotheby's, was asked to value a diamond encrusted brooch in the shape of an anchor emblazoned with the initials H & N. Given the age of the brooch and the potential significance of the initials, warning bells started to ring in his head. Keen to find out more, Downer tracked down the owners of the brooch to their home in central Europe; here they produced an old leather box containing, so they claimed, various documents and artefacts relating to Nelson.

With a thrill of anticipation, Downer turned the large iron key and opened the box. What he found was true treasure. The box had belonged to Alexander Davison, friend and trusted confidante of Lord Nelson, and it was full of beautifully preserved documents including letters to Davison from Nelson himself, Nelson's wife Fanny and his mistress, Emma Hamilton.

Enthralled, Downer was then shown a collection of objects around the castle, all belonging to Davison and commemorating such events as the battles of the Nile and Trafalgar. There was even a snuffbox made from wood carved from the main mast of *HMS Victory* herself. Finally, he was presented with an old silk purse, apparently stained with blood. Inside, Downer found 21 gold coins, the latest dated 1804, and a small, fragile piece of paper claiming that the purse and its contents had been found on Nelson when he was shot and killed at Trafalgar.

What follows makes *Nelson's Purse* a truly absorbing detective story. Combining history, biography, art and antiques it rewrites the history of one of the world's most celebrated masters and commanders.

Recommended by Peter Saxton,
Waterstone's Brentford

£20.00
ISBN: 0593051807
Published October 2004

Before *Victory* weighed anchor to begin the journey round the coast to the Thames, a shambolic new passenger joined the ship. His ill-fitting clothes were threadbare and old-fashioned. More intriguing was the ugly scar on his cheek, the result of an arrow fired by a native in the East Indies. This was Arthur William Devis: a painter of portraits and recent resident of the King's Bench prison for debtors. In his pocket was an advertisement torn from the *Morning Chronicle* offering 500 guineas for the best painting of the death of Nelson. Josiah Boydell, the printmaker who had placed the notice, wanted to emulate the commercial success of the prints made after General James Wolfe's heroic death capturing Quebec in 1759.

Devis, a man incapable of properly managing his affairs, had been dogged by debt for years. Hearing that *Victory* had reached England, he secured his release from the King's Bench, probably on the promise of Boydell's fee – which would have been easy enough as the printmaker held a sinecure at the prison. Quickly fetching his painting equipment from his lodgings in Hanover Square, Devis hurtled down to Portsmouth, trailing paint and brushes. By befriending the ship's officers in the taverns around the town he managed to secure a berth on *Victory*. It is likely that Davison, who at one point had been in the King's Bench with Devis, had a quiet word with Hardy on behalf of the artist.

To the disappointment of the people of Portsmouth, the *Victory* sailed on 11 December with Nelson's body still on board. After checking with his own physician whether his brother might be infectious, the earl had decided that the body should be left undisturbed and landed in London without fanfare – 'not knowing whether it would be corrupted and produce any disagreeable smell by being kept out of spirits so many days before the internment'. As ship's surgeon, William Beatty was far better placed to judge how fast Nelson was decomposing; and so, like everyone else, Beatty ignored the earl. With *Victory* at sea and away from the gaze of the public, he set about removing the body from the cask and performing an autopsy 'to check the progress of decay which was taking place'.

Beatty's assistants prised open the cask, releasing a rush of putrid air. Many of the witnesses, who included Devis, gagged and turned away. The corpse, which was floating upside down in a foetal position, bobbed to the surface of the brandy. After being lifted and drained, it was placed on a board and slowly, very carefully, stretched out. Some of the bones had to be broken to do this. The corpse was naked except for a white cotton shirt which was cut off and discarded. The stink was appalling; nevertheless, everyone pressed forward to see the horrific sight. The corpse's roughly shaved head made it look vulnerable and childlike. The decomposition was advanced, the skin sticky and stained the colour of walnut by the brandy. After using a sponge to wash the body, Beatty gently rubbed the face with a soft cloth. Alexander Scott, *Victory*'s chaplain, who had kept a lonely vigil by the cask, noticed sadly that his friend's features could not, 'at this distant period from his demise, be easily traced'. Exposure during the lying-in-state, everyone agreed, would be impossible.

Wielding a large knife, Beatty opened the abdomen from throat to groin in a series of short, firm movements, releasing large quantities of rancid liquid. There was a tearing sound as he pulled the flesh away from the ribcage. Using a probe fed into the body through the neat hole in the shoulder, Beatty traced the line of the ball which had killed Nelson. He patiently explained how it had travelled diagonally down through the body, fracturing the scapulae and two ribs, slicing through the left lobe of the lungs and severing the pulmonary artery before fracturing two vertebrae and lodging in the muscles of the lower right back. Here Beatty extracted the ball with a slight theatrical flourish. Surprisingly, a small portion of Nelson's blue uniform coat and some gold lace from his epaulette remained stuck to the ball, which was passed to Devis to sketch. The contents of the body cavity, except for the heart, were removed, inspected and weighed. Beatty remarked, with approval, that the organs were in excellent condition: the result, he told the spectators – perhaps looking at Devis – of moderate habits. The gutted corpse was sewn up, wrapped tightly in bandages and placed beside its organs in a lead-lined pine coffin made by Bunce, the ship's carpenter. Before it was sealed, the coffin was filled with strong spirits, 'after the ancient mode of embalming'.

That weekend was bitterly cold – so cold, the Serpentine froze in Hyde Park. The royal family opened the Christmas season at Covent Garden. Mrs Siddons and Mrs Jordan appeared together at Drury Lane. Songs to Nelson were sung in the interlude. St Paul's Cathedral was a hive of activity, with labourers building galleries and enclosures for the state funeral. Daily bulletins in the press reported *Victory*'s slow progress to London alongside advertisements for viewing positions along the funeral route.

Monday 16 December was the day appointed for the meeting at Clarges Street. William Haslewood woke with a cold, so he sent his brother to meet the earl and Davison at Emma's house, where the two men had visited often since the news of Nelson's death. They were joined there at two o'clock by John Tyson, one of Nelson's former secretaries and now a commissioner at Woolwich dockyard. Captain Blackwood had arrived earlier with the box from *Victory*. The first thing the earl and Davison noticed, as the bedroom door opened to admit them, was the blue uniform coat, stiff with blood, stretched across the mass of letters, papers, shawls and jewels strewn over the bed. Blackwood stood as they entered, acknowledging them with a nod.

Smiling bravely, Emma turned her large, green eyes towards each of the men in turn. Her mother, talking all the while, fussed about her, securing the curtains on the bed and arranging everybody on chairs with cups of tea. Emma had grown fat but she was still exceptionally beautiful. Her skin was very smooth, as pale and as perfect as the finest china, her face slightly flushed by wine and the warmth of the room. Her dark auburn hair fell in soft, loose curls across her large, full breasts. Two small crescents, the colour of rich chocolate, peeped above her thin shift. All the men tried to look elsewhere.

After some respectful words, and a stifled sob from Emma, Blackwood opened a red morocco case sitting on a table at the end of the bed. It was a moment of high drama. Reaching inside, he lifted out a group of papers and documents, some tied in bundles with pink ribbon, others sealed with wax. Everyone spotted the small flat parcel neatly wrapped and sealed in a sheet of paper. This was passed reverently to Emma, who broke the seal and tore off the wrapper, her tears falling silently. Inside was a slightly scuffed black leather pocket book. Pausing to recover her composure, Emma opened it and read the last words written in the book by Nelson. There was a prayer, followed by a statement of Lady Hamilton's services to her country while married to the British ambassador in Naples. Finally, there was a bequest:

> I leave Emma Lady Hamilton, therefore, a legacy to my King and Country, that they will give her an ample provision to maintain her rank in life. I also leave to the beneficence of my Country my adopted daughter Horatia Nelson Thompson, and I desire she will use in future the name of Nelson only. These are the only favours I ask of my King and Country at this moment, when I am going to fight their Battle. May God bless my King and Country, and all those who I hold dear. My Relations it is needless to mention they will of course be amply provided for.

When Emma had finished speaking there was a long silence. Everyone knew that Nelson had been urging the government for years to give his mistress a pension; so, despite the drama attending its composition and transmittal, and despite all the conjecture surrounding it, the codicil was hardly unexpected, nor were its contents surprising. Hardy's interpretation that it did not change the will was right. Nevertheless, this codicil would obsess Emma for the rest of her life.

It seemed inevitable that William Pitt would grant the pension now that Nelson had saved the country from defeat. No-one in the room knew, however, that Pitt was dying. Davison offered to send a copy of the codicil to the Prince of Wales to muster royal support. Emma's effect on the prince was well known – indeed, Nelson had once feared she would become 'a whore to the rascal'.

The remaining contents of the case were then examined and a list made. This list, which survives in the British Library, reveals a small and strangely affecting group of objects. Alongside a copy of Nelson's will, some old codicils and 'papers unknown', were the seals from his desk used on the letters they had all received over the years. There was also a compass, a ring; some 'coins found in Sardinia', a picture and two pocket watches. 'A medal' may have been the gold medal taken from Nelson's neck as he lay dying. If so, it was passed to Davison.

There were also a worn banknote case holding £12 in cash and two purses holding coins. It seems from the surviving manuscript that, at first, 'contents unknown' was written beside the purses; but then, apparently, a quick tally was made, the coins spilling noisily across the polished table. One of the purses – presumably some form of pouch – was made of leather. It must have been tucked away in Nelson's desk rather than carried with him, for it contained no less than 79 gold guineas and one shilling, making £83 in total – a weighty sum worth over £4,000 today. But it was the other purse that attracted most attention. Later described as 'Nelson's pocket purse', this was made of woven green silk and was distinctly, and freshly, stained in blood. It held the far smaller sum of

£17 5s 0d in an unspecified number of gold and silver coins. This purse and all the money were entrusted to Davison. The leather pouch disappeared for ever. Before the men headed back out into the snow, the earl arranged to call on Davison the next day with Haslewood to discuss his brother's estate.

As soon as he reached Charles Street, the earl wrote to Haslewood. 'The box', he revealed, with evident relief, 'contained duplicates of the will & codicils we had before, I don't recollect any thing new . . . the memorandum book, is a short account of his proceedings since he left England last, up to the day of battle & concludes with recommending L.H to Government – you will see all tomorrow.' The earl now knew that even if his brother's last wishes were honoured, they could not affect his new fortune. The issue of a pension for Emma was one for the government, not for his family. It was nothing to worry about after all.

Before the meeting at St James's Square Davison wrote to the Prince of Wales as he had promised Emma. He enclosed a copy of Nelson's 'legacy . . . abstracted from his journal' and a note 'of a private nature' he had received that morning from Emma, 'whose sufferings poor woman are beyond expression'. Emma's note lavished praise on the prince and was clearly intended, with Davison's connivance, to be sent on to him at Brighton.

Davison received Haslewood and the earl in the back drawing room of 9 St James's Square, overlooking the narrow garden which stretched behind the house to the stables, offices and coach houses of Ormonde Yard. The garden was planted with small, bare fruit trees. A slow thaw made the whole scene look drab and grey, with piles of snow, blackened by soot, banked untidily against the walls. In brilliant contrast, the drawing room was filled with warmth and light. Nelson's purse lay on a table. After returning the pocket book to the earl, Davison asked a clerk to make a proper account of all the cash and coins found among Nelson's belongings.

The clerk called this document simply 'Money, Coins in Lord Nelson's Pocket Purse &c when killed'. It reveals a total sum slightly larger than the one hastily calculated the day before, apparently combining the money found in both purses:

[Tue]s day	90 Guineas -		94 10 –
17th [Decembe]r 1805	9 Half do -		4. 14 6
St James's Square	3 – 7/-	1. 1	
	Silver		2: 0 6
Contents of			
Lord Nelsons Purse in his Red		102. 6. 0	
[Case]			
[Bank note case]		12	
			£114.6

Haslewood and the earl witnessed the document before hurrying off to prove Nelson's will, their concerns over the final codicil allayed. All the money was left with Davison, who folded the document and tucked it into the purse. He then carried the purse downstairs to his office, placing it in a large iron strongbox which he locked with an elaborate key kept in his waistcoat pocket. He had an important meeting to attend at the Treasury.

The next morning, Wednesday 18 December, Davison left the house early to cross the square. Again the fog was so heavy that he felt cocooned from the rest of the city. There was a soft yellow tear in the gloom where the financier Abraham Goldsmid had put up lamps to mourn his friend. No houses fronted onto the square on the south side; instead, the entrances led into the rear of houses facing onto Pall Mall. The unmarked door on which Davison tapped his cane was opened by a young footman, who bowed and took the visitor's coat. Striding through the house, past the clerks' room and the partners' room, Davison soon reached the main banking hall of his bank, Alexander Davison, Noel, Templer & Co.

Davison & Co. had been on Pall Mall for only two years, but in that short time it had acquired all the characteristics of the older, better-established banks in the West End. A feeling of timeless solidity, dependability and quiet industry permeated its rooms and the people within them. The banking hall had a polished wooden floor below a white plastered ceiling bordered by a simple classical pattern and supported on eight elegant oak pillars. The size of a comfortable drawing room, it felt smaller because running across it was a mahogany counter topped by a brightly polished brass railing and a row of oil lamps with dark green glass shades. Behind the counter were a desk for the chief cashier, stools for the clerks and wooden pigeonholes stuffed with papers. A large wall-mounted clock occasionally chimed sonorously. There were two fireplaces in the hall, one for the clerks and a better and larger one for the customers. On the other side of Pall Mall, Carlton House, the town residence of the Prince of Wales, loomed through the fog.

After a brief discussion on business and the grave news of a victory for Bonaparte over the Austrians and Russians at somewhere called Austerlitz, Davison presented his chief cashier with a bill for £114 6s 0d drawn on himself. The cashier was told to credit the amount to Lord Nelson's account as 'cash found in his red box'.

Davison returned home to a letter from Brighton. The Prince of Wales assured him that 'did it depend upon me, there would not be a wish, a desire of our ever-to-be-lamented and much loved friend, as well as adored hero, that I would not consider as a solemn obligation upon his friends and his country to fulfil'. In other words, the matter of Emma's pension was not his problem.

John Tyson searched the Thames estuary for three days in his yacht from Woolwich. Then, early on Sunday 22 December, the mist lifted to reveal *Victory* anchored peacefully near Sheerness, as if placed there gently overnight. When a strong gale blew up, however, it was only with the greatest difficulty, and some danger, that Tyson was able to clamber on board the towering warship. Lashed by squalls of freezing rain and with the ship pitching heavily, two coffins were winched across onto *Victory*, swinging so wildly on the ropes that they almost smashed to bits. Entering the great cabin, Tyson's eyes fell immediately on the long pine box. Around it, grim-faced and silent, stood the ship's officers, their shadows leaping about the cabin in the swaying light of the lanterns. William Chevailler stood a little behind them. Without ceremony, the box was prised opened and two marines lifted out the corpse, wrapped in its soaking bandages. It looked very small. As the marines paused to allow the bundle to drain, the cabin filled with the sweet smell of camphor.

The corpse and the parcels holding the organs were placed on the dining table, which William had draped with a Union Jack. Beatty stepped forward and started gently to remove the bandaging, careful to avoid lifting off the marbled, flaying skin. When naked, the corpse was dried. For the last time and with tears in his eyes, Nelson's Sicilian valet, Gaetano Spedillo, dressed his master in shirt, stockings, breeches and waistcoat. Alexander Scott, looking pale and tired, read a short prayer before the officers took farewell of their commander, each in his own way. Then the corpse was placed in the elaborate wooden coffin that had been made from the mast of *L'Orient*, the French flagship destroyed at the battle of the Nile. This was lowered into an outer lead casket which Bunce soldered shut, sealing it for ever.

On Christmas Eve, extracts from Nelson's will appeared in the London newspapers. 'The only legacies', noticed the *Morning Chronicle*, 'to persons not of Lord Nelson's family are to Lady Hamilton, to Mr Davison, to Mr Haslewood, Captain Hardy, to Miss Horatia Nelson Thompson, to Mr John Scott, [and] to the Rev. A. J. Scott.' Most interest was inevitably focused on Nelson's legacies to his estranged wife Fanny and to his mistress Emma. Few people noticed one intriguing detail buried deep within the document: 'I give and bequeath to Alexander Davison, of St. James's Square, in the County of Middlesex, Esquire: my Turkish Gun, Scimitar and Canteen.'

*

My part in this story begins in June 2002 when I visited a Sotheby's office on the continent, as I often did in my endless search for jewels to auction. There was nothing unusual about the trip; certainly no sign that I was about to come across something that would change my life. The jewels I saw were the normal run-of-the-mill pieces: some old, some not; some precious, more not, though all of course priceless to their owners. Describing and valuing the jewels which were placed in front of me one by one, I tried to be as helpful and as tactful as I could. The owners responded as they did the world over, sometimes with surprise and pleasure but as often with disappointment, even resentment, their hopes of a fortune dashed. Nevertheless, as the hours passed, I steadily reaped a small harvest of jewels to take back to sell in London. So the company would be pleased in any event.

Late on, as my thoughts drifted towards my flight home, a pleasant middle-aged couple arrived with just one piece to show me. It was large brooch designed as an anchor, sparkling with plump, watery white diamonds, all cut thickly in the old antique style. The diamonds were mounted in a sandwich of silver and honey-coloured gold. Dulled now by tarnish, the pure whiteness of the silver would once have flattered the diamonds, displaying them to their best glittering advantage, while the gold gave the jewel strength and richness. The diamonds, which I quickly gauged at over 17 carats, had the brilliance and the purity of the finest Indian stones, mined long before the great discoveries in South Africa in the 1880s. Turning the brooch over, I saw that its pin had an old lead repair. Otherwise the back was as beautifully finished as the front, a sign of excellence and rare in later reproductions. There were no maker's marks or hallmarks – but I would not have expected any on a jewel of that age.

The style of setting, the type and the cut of the diamonds, the *feel* of the jewel all told me it had been made early in the nineteenth century. As such it was undoubtedly a rare survivor, a glittering relic of a lost age. Most important diamond jewels from that far-off era have gone for ever, their stones recycled, recut and reset as fashions changed and fortunes fluctuated. I valued the brooch at over £100,000. But something else absolutely, uniquely, distinguished this jewel. Something which made me catch my breath. Something so improbable, impossible even, that it was hard to grasp, far too much to hope for. On either side of the anchor clung a small initial, each perfectly drawn in tiny diamonds. Two letters that promised everything yet revealed nothing. Two letters. *H* and *N*.

In the course of ten years as a specialist at Sotheby's I had seen thousands of jewels. Some were spectacularly valuable, some worthless; but the thrill of not knowing what might turn up next, the hope that a great discovery could be around the next corner, never diminished. Anyone in the auction business would say the same. Yet of all those jewels, those that I remember now I remember not because of their value but because of the stories they told. Jewels, especially the antique ones, carry an extraordinary emotional resonance. They hold the memory of cold metal on warm, scented skin; the candlelit gaze of a long-dead lover or a stolen kiss in a moon-drenched garden. Everyone it touches turns to dust, yet the jewel itself remains unblemished, an inviolable fragment of beauty, a silent witness to history tumbling through the centuries.

Now here I was on a warm summer's day, the faint noise of traffic and the happy babble of a café drifting through the open windows, stumbling towards the moment of discovery. Lying cold in my hand was a 200-year-old diamond brooch designed as an anchor and mounted with the initials of Britain's greatest naval hero. I tried to remain calm, professional, but my mind was racing. The tremor in my voice must have betrayed my excitement. How, I asked, turning the jewel over, its diamonds flashing brilliantly, did such a thing come to be in your family? Then, for the first time, I heard the name of the owner's English ancestor: Alexander Davison, 'Lord Nelson's best friend'.

The name Davison echoed in my head as, excited and intrigued, I returned to London. I knew the legend of Nelson, of course, as most of us do. The one arm, the one eye, the love affair, the death, the monument, the hero, the myth. But who was Alexander Davison? Where did he fit in? Why did he own such an extravagant relic? I soon found him. He was in all the biographies, running like a thread through the well-worn story. Davison was described as a confidant, an adviser, an *homme d'affaires*, a banker, an agent – but yes, above all, as Nelson's friend, perhaps his closest. Yet he was over-shadowed by the many more glamorous figures who surrounded Nelson, relegated, it seemed, to the status of a slightly roguish, even embarrassing, footnote. He was a remote, elusive figure. An outsider. A civilian in a military world. This unobtrusiveness was surprising, for Davison left a large legacy, far greater than most in Nelson's circle of friends.

Over one hundred letters from Nelson to Davison were published as early as the 1840s. Most are now in the British Library, while many of Davison's replies are kept in the National Maritime Museum at Greenwich. A cursory reading of them revealed no mention of the anchor brooch – nor could I realistically have hoped that it would. The NMM also holds a remarkable hoard of Nelsonian treasures from Davison's personal collection, bequeathed to the nation by his son in 1873. These are displayed in a gallery devoted to Nelson, the museum's busiest. They include a portrait of the admiral by an artist called Lemuel Abbott, a brass cannon captured at the battle of Copenhagen and a fine marble bust of Nelson by the neo-classical sculptor John Flaxman. Drifting round the gallery with the other tourists on my first visit there, I also noticed an exotic-looking sabre with a gold hilt designed as a crocodile. The scabbard was engraved:

This SCYMETER together with a GUN and CANTEEN were presented by the GRAND SIGNIOR to Horatio Viscount Nelson and by WILL bequeathed to his Friend Alexander Davison 10th May 1803.

The sabre looked uncomfortable in the scabbard, for it clearly didn't fit. These were disparate, isolated objects, the invisible cord of ownership that had bound them together broken and lost. I needed more. For the anchor to achieve its potential at auction, it needed to capture the public's imagination; and to do that, it had to tell its story. I needed to understand how Davison had acquired it, why he had it, why it had survived hidden away for so long. When the owners said they had a few of Davison's papers hidden away, I jumped at the chance to examine them. These might reveal a mention of the anchor in a family letter or a note of it in a dusty inventory. Something, anything. A few months later I went back; but this time I visited the owners at home.

The drive from the airport took over two hours, through a cold, empty landscape now dappled with snow. The village itself was undistinguished, much the same as the others I'd driven through and, like them, apparently deserted. Then, by an improbably large church, the clusters of small, neat houses parted to reveal an incredible fairy-tale castle with brightly painted turrets and sheer castellated walls. Its most striking feature was a gigantic white tower which rose up from the heart of this extraordinary spectacle like a great anchored rocket. The castle was protected by a wide moat and surrounded, in the English style, by a landscaped park. Only the cawing of the rooks, perched like black smudges in the bare branches of the beech trees, disturbed the complete wintry silence. It was spellbinding. Did Rosalie Davison feel the same as, newly wed, she stepped nervously out of her carriage after her long journey from England to stand where I stood now, to gaze as I gazed?

Inside I was led through a medieval stone-vaulted hall. On a wall above the stairs was a huge canvas of a red-coated officer on horseback. The officer was haughtily reviewing a line of troops. 'Respectfully presented', the plaque on the elegantly carved and gilded frame announced, 'to Lieut. Col. Alex Davison by the Loyal Britons Volunteer Infantry March 1806.' Hanging by Davison's side was the scabbard I had seen at the National Maritime Museum, though the sword in it was quite different. The next room had an elaborately carved ceiling, painted in the Renaissance style and hung with Venetian chandeliers. Tall windows overlooked the moat and the park. On the long, highly polished mahogany dining table was an old box brought down from the castle attics for me to look at. Covered in faded red morocco leather with scrolling brass handles at each end, it bore on its top, embossed in gold, the inscription: ALEX^R. DAVISON ESQ^R. COMMISSARY GENERAL.

The box was locked, but the elaborate iron key turned easily enough. The inside was lined with rich green velvet and hand-coloured marbled paper. It was overflowing with letters and papers. I felt a rush of expectation, like a child the night before Christmas. I had no plan. I simply scooped the papers out, feeling the weight and grainy texture of their thick, creamy pages, and began to read them. As the minutes and then hours passed, the archive settled into two distinct parts. The first would loosely be termed the formal papers. There were legal and financial documents, full of incomprehensible numbers. There were also lists of the men in Nelson's warships, with long forgotten names like John Jolly, Robert Dwyer, Luke Murphy, Jeremiah Reily, Joseph Murray and David Brady. On one, otherwise insignificant, roughly torn wrapper was written in a neat hand: 'Lord Nelson's last Memorandum Book up to the 21st of October 1805 containing a Codicil to his Will written a short time before the Commencement of the Action – Sealed up by Capt Hardy in presence of the Revd Mr Scott – who has also annexed his seal.'

There was no time to make sense of these documents, even if I could. So I turned to the remaining papers, which were largely personal letters. Most were written on thick sheets of paper with Britannia watermarks. Some were folded into envelopes, with their wax seals, smudged and pressed with a variety of crests, still clinging resolutely to them. The letters were in a variety of hands, all largely indecipherable at first to my inexperienced eye. I tried to arrange them by writer, scanning them for clues, looking at signatures and addresses. Small piles began forming on the table in front of me. As I grew familiar with the writing, scattered phrases began lifting off the pages to swim into focus, their meaning still a mystery.

My poor dear father is no more, god bless you . . . I am all to him in the world and god almighty knows he is all to me . . . I have not had a line from him this age I am sure he writes who can be so wicked as to take my letters . . . I am now distrustful and fearful of my own shadow . . . once the victory took fire near the powder magazine the whole of the terrified crew rund up the riggen . . . I hope to get at their fleet . . . I love him I would do anything in the world to convince him of my affection . . . one fortnight of joy and happiness I have had for years of pain . . . I am gone nor do I wish to live . . . this dreadful weight of most wretched misery . . .

Voices released from their morocco-bound prison after two hundred years began to fill the room. They were hesitant at first but soon they pressed forward, each eager to be heard above the others. A glorious babble washed over me: a jumble of joy, laughter, love, pain, treachery, anger and death. Opening the box was like breaking a spell and eavesdropping on a conversation stopped long ago. I felt like an intruder and a little sad.

The park outside the windows had disappeared into darkness when I finally sat back, my eyes aching and my head full of broken fragments of speech. On the table were over seven hundred pages of letters and documents. The letters from Nelson to Davison were in a bold, open hand, the ink running thickly over the page. The last had been written on *Victory* just a week before the battle of Trafalgar. There were letters from Nelson's mistress, Emma Lady Hamilton. These were in a gratifyingly apposite style, her large, loose hand scattering the words across the page in lines sometimes so precipitously slanted that it seemed they might slide off the page altogether. They looked exactly what they were: letters written propped up in bed. Remarkably, there were also over seventy letters written to Davison by Frances Nelson, Nelson's wife. Fanny's hand was quite different from Emma's: small, neat and tight. She wrote with great care and attention. Yet this formal style disguised feelings every bit as passionate as those of her famous rival. Fanny's letters would be a revelation.

The papers in the box were just the beginning. Scattered around that remarkable castle, from top to bottom, hidden away in cabinets and drawers, was an astonishing treasure trove of Nelson relics, all preserved untouched from Alexander Davison's collection. There was another sword with a gold crocodile hilt set with a perfectly painted enamel of the battle of the Nile. Unlike the one at the National Maritime Museum, this sword was straight-bladed, its steel still razor sharp. There were also medals in gold, silver and copper, all in mint condition, all similarly decorated. On one side was a female figure standing on a cliff gazing out to sea holding a shield bearing a bust of Nelson; the other side depicted the battle of the Nile below the motto ALMIGHTY GOD HAS BLESSED HIS MAJESTY'S ARMS. Running around the edge of each medal was this inscription: FROM ALEX[R.] DAVISON ESQ[R.] S[T.] JAMES'S SQUARE – A TRIBUTE OF REGARD. Close to the medals was a small wooden snuff box. A gold plaque on its lid, no bigger than a postage stamp, told me the box was made from *Victory*'s main mast, 'close to which the immortal NELSON fell'. There were richly bound books from Naples, rare guns and a pair of magnificent wine-coolers from the Derby porcelain factory, flamboyantly painted with Nelson's coat of arms and a colourful profusion of Egyptian symbols: palm trees, pyramids, obelisks and sphinxes. Hanging on one wall was a heavy, dangerous-looking sabre. Beneath it was a label. 'This sword belonged to Lord Nelson', it read, helpfully. The hilt of the sabre was decorated with the head of Medusa and a cap of liberty. The dull, grey blade was etched to imitate watered silk, and decorated in gold Islamic script. It was unmistakably the sabre hanging by Davison's side in the painting on the stairs. Surely this sabre would fit the scabbard with the presentation inscription on display at the National Maritime Museum? What had happened here? How had sabre and scabbard become separated?

I knew I had stumbled into something quite extraordinary. This was not a lost collection, because no-one had ever looked for it or missed it. Somehow these papers and objects had slipped from history, lying undisturbed in that castle as time swirled past. Then, as I prepared to leave, my head spinning, one last thing was placed in my hand. It was a green woven silk purse, apparently stained with blood. The purse felt hefty with gold. With a lurch I knew what this had to be. I returned to the table. The purse was about 10 inches long and shaped like a tube with a tassel on either end. Coins entered it through a 2-inch horizontal slit halfway along. Two steel rings, each apparently covered in fine strands of hair, were then evidently slid down to the ends of the purse, gathering the material and capturing the contents. One end of the purse in front of me clearly bulged with coins. The blood was dispersed across the purse but with a concentration in one large stain towards the middle, which the British press later described as tear-shaped.

Incredibly, the owners had never opened the purse. Very gently I parted the iron rings, opened the slit and felt gingerly inside. One by one I removed twenty-one gold coins with the tips of my fingers: eight guineas, six half-guineas and seven third-guineas. The earliest coin was dated 1772 and the latest 1804. Together the coins were worth £14 to Nelson. There was also a small, folded piece of paper tucked deep within the purse. I eased this out very carefully using the steel tongs I always carried with me to examine loose diamonds. The paper left a trail of dust behind it. One-quarter of this fragile document was missing; but I could read the title: 'Money, Coins in Lord Nelson's Pocket, Purse &c when Killed'. There was an incomplete date: ' . . . sday 17th . . . 1805 St Jam . . . Square' and two names, presumably witnesses: 'Wm. Haslewood and Lord Nelson'. This was confusing. Wasn't Nelson dead? The manuscript was an account of the money in the purse. Yet it listed many more coins than were before me and a total sum of £114 6s 0d. What had become of the rest of the money?

The fragment of paper had barely survived its 200-year journey to me in the darkness of the purse. Yet, incredibly, it seemed to confirm that this commonplace object was with

Nelson when he died on *Victory* at around four o'clock in the afternoon on 21 October 1805. Holding it felt like touching him. Why was the purse with Davison? Why had he been allowed to keep it? How did he get so close? Everything pointed towards a far deeper relationship between him and Nelson than had ever been hinted at. My visit to the castle had only deepened the mystery. At the heart of this puzzle, the key to it perhaps, was the enigmatic figure of Alexander Davison. Who was he?

OH, PLAY THAT THING

BY RODDY DOYLE

Roddy Doyle shows in sparkling style that he has not lost his touch in *Oh, Play that Thing*, the eagerly awaited sequel to *A Star Called Henry*.

We left Henry Smart on the run from his Republican paymasters. Having fled from Dublin to Liverpool, he eventually arrives in America and negotiates the obstacles of immigration. It's 1924, New York. The location may have shifted, but the voice of Henry Smart is unmistakable and we are plunged right back into the life of this irrepressible character.

After several jobs, he lands one carrying sandwich boards. Business booms, especially once he discovers he can carry smuggled hooch behind the boards to the speakeasies – one way round Prohibition! He branches out on his own though, and the mob soon comes after him. Henry's on the run again, destination Chicago. Enter, Louis Armstrong. Louis' music is revolutionising the place but it hasn't broken every barrier. There are still places where a black man can't go. He needs a white man to accompany him and Henry becomes that man.

Roddy Doyle established himself with the Barrytown trilogy (*The Commitments*, *The Snapper*, *The Van*,) which chronicled modern everyday Irish life. He won the Booker Prize in 1993 with *Paddy Clarke Ha Ha Ha*. By now established as one of the best writers of the generation, Doyle then embarked upon his far-reaching trilogy, *The Last Roundup*, of which *A Star Called Henry* is the first volume. In that, he magically combined the role of storyteller with historian, a task he continues in *Oh, Play that Thing*, to great effect.

Doyle is a master at creating atmosphere: as Louis starts to play, we feel the hot, sultry night, see those pursed lips, those rolling eyes and hear that deep moody jazz for ourselves. Just what lies in store for us in volume three?

**Recommended by Lindsey Russell,
Waterstone's Macclesfield**

£16.99
ISBN: 0224074369
Published September 2004

At Last.

Dead eyes. Washed blue, red veins turned to grey. Old man's bristle; cracked, dry lips – all grey. Dried skin, dirt in the corners of the mouth. I turned away.

I got to know hard work again. I handled boxes in one of the packing houses. I came home each night with hands raw and screaming from the brine that seeped into the box wood, came home with men exactly like me, proud, silent and flaked; we tried to keep a straight path through the tiredness. These men were Polish, mostly, some Lithuanians, Slovaks, and others willing to work for less than the ones who'd been there longer. They spoke the English they were getting from their kids.
    —Son of a beech.
    —Boy, is hot.
    —I'll say.
And I followed them back, and they followed me, every morning, through the Halsted Street gate, past the hundreds who stood there, waiting for us to die or strike; over the crossings, miles of tracks, a crazy mess of switches, alert for rolling trucks and engines, the air around us wet with slaughter, a stink that caught the throat and tongue, rich and sometimes sickening; nearer, into the big howl, the cries, the river of that day's pigs and cattle, the drovers among them, on horseback – there was money in this business – to the packing

house, six days a week, seven o'clock till seven, and sometimes, when the trains came fast and full, it was dark at both ends of the working day.

I was like the men I walked beside, dinner pails brushing against our overalls, like hair across a drum, the same dinner every day, a poor-boy sandwich, onions, cheese, lard, cut big by Mrs Grobnik. I was humping boxes and huge hams sewn into oiled paper across the cellar floor, through a quarter-inch of icy water; bending and pushing, grabbing and stacking, counting the minutes without thinking about them, hating it, but knowing it was work, ignoring pain, the world outside the work, the bellows and howls from the pens at the other end of the plant; smiling grimly at going-home time as the whistle rose in pitch and volume, standing straight, turning away from stacks, machinery, carcasses, as the whistle's order began to dip and quickly fade; walking home, past men like us, and women, clocking in, swapping jokes learnt years before.

—How those pigs today?
—Boy, they bleed.
—Catch the squeal?
—Too fast to catch.

And home, together and alone. Through the streets of quick-built frame houses, all two storeys – none of the high tenements – all colours already fading, smothered, eaten by the smoke that dropped from the packing-house chimneys. Over bridges that leaned across the gullies and stinking creeks that had cut grass prairie not so long ago. The water looked like settling lava – I'd seen mice and chickens running on it. Across dead country that was nothing yet, bare spaces that would soon be gone. Through square miles of new-built, falling houses. Home, to wives and kids, husbands and kids, mothers, fathers, aunts; along sidewalks, where there were any, rotten planks five and six feet above the unpaved road.

I was there, in the swing, like these men and women. But I didn't go home. I didn't have one. I had a room. I lay and woke there, with six other men. I walked slowly through this patch of Back o' the Yards, to Mrs Grobnik's house. Up two steps, through the boarded-up porch that slept five men.

—Mees-ter Smarhht.

I was Henry Smart. I was back again, and working hard.

—Mees-ter Smarhht.

—Mrs Grobnik.

—Hard day?

—The usual, Mrs Grobnik.

—Yes, hard. Eat in, eat out tonight, Mees-ter Smarhht?

—Out, Mrs Grobnik.

—Again, out! Out! When in? Nev-errr.

She had a niece she wanted me to look at, a girl fresh in from Akron.

—Nice girl, big bones. For you.

She wouldn't believe I wasn't Polish.

—Smarhht-nik, yes?

—No, I told her, again. —Just Smart.

It was a ritual by now, daily ambush on the stairs, every time a step gave out the creak that only she could hear.

—Smarhht-ka, yes?

—No.

I'd never made it past her door. I'd skipped every step, one a day, for weeks, till I'd hopped them all, but still she heard. And now she grabbed my shoulders. I'd carried her up the first flight before I felt her nails through my shirt.

—Ah now, Missis Grobnik.

—Poh-lish!

—No, I said. —American.

—And father? she screamed.

—American.

—But mother!

—American.

—So grandfather!

—Don't know.

—A-hah!

—Irish. I think.

I'd stopped on the landing, so she could get down off my back, to the black patch on the once-green lino.

—Irish, she laughed. —Hear him, Mees-ter Grobnik?

83

He was around somewhere, the husband, although I'd never seen him. I'd hear her call him, screaming questions that he never answered. But he was there – a stiff door being shoved into place, a trunk moved in the attic, the tied dog's excitement as he approached.

I shut the door on her cheerful whine.

There were men asleep and lying on mattresses. I nodded at those that looked. I took the basin, brought it to the yard, filled it, brought it back, and placed it on the room's one chair. I dropped my face into the water and left it there, till I knew the day was gone. I got my head up, filled my lungs, felt the cold on my skin like it was new. Then I dealt with the rest of the dirt, knocked it off, went at it with a hard brush, watched by lads who didn't really get it – it was three, four days to Saturday night. I put on the suit, polished the boots. I was the only man in the room with spare clothes, and they knew well not to touch them. No tiredness now, no lost years or fear. I was ready to ramble.

—Out!

—Yes, Missis Grobnik.

—Out!

I stepped out, every night. I walked. I covered the city, street by street, acre by acre. I sniffed and took in the town-wide stinks – meat, metal, big wind from wide spaces, and the smells that marked the districts, neighbourhoods, the old countries. I leaned on brick corners, knew when not to rest against other bricks. I got to know the Loop, crossed every street and alley. I looked for the eyes of ownership, the weight of guns. I knew when I was measured or could walk unnoticed. I was careful.

But it was good. There was room here. I strayed across the river, north, and west, and south. I walked and crossed the names and numbers. Huron, Erie, Ontario. West 31st, 32nd. Harrison, Jefferson, Polk. I copped the speakeasies as I strolled past, the sudden fumes, the snatch of song as a door opened somewhere. I spotted the gang hotels, the men and cars parked outside, the cop shops and brothels, all there, all in place, all avoidable. Crossing the street was enough, turning a corner was an old place left behind. I listened for talk and gunshots. The shots were there, some nights, and charging cars and more shots, but always far away. No one ran for cover. Business as usual; let them at it. It was the big city. Things could be distant here.

The neighbourhoods were easy. Big chunks of built-up prairie that a man could stay lost in, if he was quick and very quietly flamboyant. No good fedora – not since Sweet Afton – no Darrow suspenders, not even here, the home of Clarence Darrow. I could walk past and through – there was space for a man – without stepping aside or begging pardon. The Irish patches weren't as Irish, the Italians weren't as Mediterranean – there was room for America here. I wasn't stupid or sentimental. There were plenty of fuckers, hot for murder and profit; but there was room for big elbows here. A man could turn and walk away, and walk as fast and as slow and as far as he wanted. I roamed the night. I got back for the two hours' sleep, all I wanted, on the mattress I shared with a chap on the night shift, a Slovak I'd only met once.

I was ready for Mrs Grobnik's call before she opened her mouth.

—Riy-isssse, shiy-nnnne!

She was at the bottom of the stairs, waking the stiffs of the house.

—In, Mees-ter Smarhht?

—In, Missis Grobnik.

—Away-ke?

—Yes, Missis Grobnik.

—Hon-gry?

—Yeah.

—You betcha. Out all night.

Out all night, and I was always heading south.

I'd stay away for days, sometimes the week and another day or two, but I always went back south. And, to get there, I went east, and north, to State Street. And, when I wandered that way, I took my Clarence Darrows and I let them twang. Here a man could wear lilac as he walked into the blues, past the pig-ear-sandwich truck, around the sidewalk dice game.

Through new smells and meat goods – *Chitterlings, Spare Ribs, Neck Bones* – past pool halls and stores – *Plaids, Stripes, Checks*. I strolled the Stroll, past newsies flogging the *Defender*, and the open door of the Greater Lily Baptist Church, next door to the fight club. And I felt the freedom I'd really never known before. Because there was no past now waiting to jump. I had to be careful but there was nothing behind my back; it was all ahead. The place was wild, and as new as I was.

I waited for Dora.

At last. I wasn't Irish any more. The first time I heard it, before I was properly listening, I knew for absolute sure. It took me by the ears and spat on my forehead, baptised me. There was a whole band of men on the bandstand, and a little woman at the piano, all thumping and blowing their lives away. Two horns, a trombone, tuba, banjo, drums, filling the world with their glorious torment. There were two trumpets blowing but the spit on my forehead came from only one man's. I looked at him through the human steam – it was too hot there for sweat – and I knew it.

I was a Yank.

At last.

It was like nothing I'd heard before, nothing like the American songs that Piano Annie had played on my spine in Dublin, before I'd had to run. This was free and wordless and the man with the trumpet was driving it forward without ever looking back. It was furious, happy and lethal; it killed all other music. It was new, like me.

—You got a name, honey?

There was a gorgeous thing beside me, checking out the fabric of my suit. The suit was old – three years since I'd bought it – but the collar was hours-old new.

—I've got several, I told her.

—That supposed to impress me?

—No, I said. —When I'm impressing you, you won't have to ask.

—Now ain't you a man.

—And ain't you a woman.

I was recovering. I was Henry Smart and there was a woman here who was interested in getting to know me. I looked at her properly.

She wasn't black. She wasn't white. She was new too, invented seconds before and plonked in front of me. Just for me, the new American.

But the trumpet was butting at me; I had to look. She wasn't put off or put out. I could feel her breath, and it was new too, made of things I hadn't tasted. It was stroking my neck.

—Who's that? I said.

I nodded at the stage.

—You don't know him? she said.

—No.

—He the man all you white folks come down here to see.

—Who is he?

She told me. I learnt all his names that night. Dipper. Gate. Gatemouth. Dippermouth. Daddy. Pops. Little Louie. Laughing Louie. Louis Armstrong. The names danced among the crazy lights that jumped from the mirror ball above the dance floor. He was dancing now as he played, as if his legs were tied to the notes that jumped from the bell of his horn. His steps were crazy but he was in control. He was puppet and master, god and disciple, a one-man band in perfect step with the other players surrounding him. His lips were bleeding – I saw drops fall like notes to his patent leather shoes – but he was the happiest man on earth.

—Any man worth a damn need more than one name, said the woman. —Ain't that the truth?

—I've had a few, I told her.

—Well now, drop one on me.

—Henry.

—More.

—S.

—And?

—Smart.

—Henry S. Smart?

—Hello.

—What's with the S?

—So.

—Henry So Smart?

—You're looking at him.

—Well, my oh my.

I was Henry Smart again – no more running and hiding.

—What's your own name, baby? I asked her.

I could say *baby* now; I was American.

—What day is it? she said.

—It might be Monday, I said. —I'm not sure.

—Then I might be Dora, she said. —I'm not sure.

The band stopped suddenly and the man with the trumpet yelled.

—Oh, play that thing!

Then the band was off again, all back on crazy tracks, heading for the same place by routes that were all their own. And the man wiped blood from his lips with the back of his big hand; he put the horn back to his mouth, hopped tracks and never crashed.

There was a beautiful woman close beside me but I couldn't take my eyes off Louis Armstrong.

—Ain't he the blowin'est? she said.

I looked at her now. She really was something.

—Want to try the Bunny Hug, Henry S.?

—Sounds good.

—Is good.

And I danced with her. I was dancing with a woman for the first time in my life. She was wrapped around me, even though we hadn't touched. Then my hands found her back and hers found mine. And we danced right out of the music, to the back edge of the dance floor, but we kept ourselves trapped in the rhythm, and danced right back in again, under the lights and trumpet drops. And we stood there as the music stopped, gut to magnificent gut. Her elbows rested on my hips and she tapped my arse with her sequined pocketbook.

—Well. Now.

—What do they call you on Tuesdays? I asked her.

—Why?

—I'd like to know your name when I wake up beside you.

I hadn't spoken in months; it was great.

—Oh now, she said. —Where's your ambition, Henry S.? I'll be Ethel on Wednesday.

—Fair enough, I said. —Ethel it is.

She grabbed a handful of my shirt and we walked out under a canopy that stretched forever in front of us, and out, into light, hot rain, to State Street and the rest of the new world.

I asked her a question.

—Is this going to cost me?

—Nothing but a whole lot of sweat, said Dora.

Jesus, though, it was good to be wet and alive. Less than a week in Chicago and I was holding down a job, a room and the makings of a night of serious riding. I was clean and clean-shaven, going nowhere far. I was on solid ground, strolling through air full of the caressing rain that couldn't kill the rich stink of the new-dead cattle and pigs, and the live ones in the stockyards that knew their hours were numbered; I could hear them from miles away – the music couldn't kill them. There was money in this air and music coming from every open door, and Armstrong's music followed us all the way, shoving and pulling, rubbing our shoulders.

Oh, play that thing.

No old villages here. This was a city. Manhattan was an island; I'd walked it side to side. There was no walking this one. Chicago had room. It was a great port, a thousand miles from the sea, surrounded by all of America. All trains led to Chicago but I'd spent two years, more, getting here. And here I was, alive again, young again, new.

We crossed a hopping street. We didn't talk as we turned off State, one more Bronzeville block to Dora's house and a room three flights up.

There was no one else there.

—Way I like it.

She kicked off her shoes. They landed where she wanted them.

Oh, play that thing.

We hit the mattress – the room had five; hers was the only one on a bed, on castors that took us all over the floor. By the time we slid out onto the floor, Tuesday was well spent.

—Well my, she said.

I was probably out of a brand new job; I didn't know, and I didn't care.

She sat up and grabbed a blanket from the bed. There was a red curtain hanging to our left, making two rooms of the one; the kitchen – a sink and stove – was behind it.

—Well, Mister Henry S., she said as she covered us. —Long time since you did that trick with a lady.

—What makes you think that? I said.

—Oh now, she said. —I can tell. You went at it for near two days, boy.

—You were with me all the way, baby.

Bayay-bee.

—Ain't just the hours, said Dora. —It the way you fill them. Fucked for two days but you came in seven seconds flat.

She was right. It had been a long time since I'd buried myself in a woman's hair, since I'd rubbed my hand on someone else's skin. And her skin; she was gorgeous, away from the club's mirror ball and the music that had made all women gorgeous. It was good to be alive. I was relaxing for the first real time since I'd left Ireland. I could lie back and feel only the tiredness. I was looking at her window, taking in the sounds from the street below us and streets beyond, sounds that travelled miles to die at our feet.

—I've been here five days, I told her. —And there hasn't been one second when I haven't heard music.

—Music being born every minute in this city, she said. —I love it.

—Are you not from here?

—No one from Chicago, Henry S., she said. —No coloured, anyway.

—Where are you from?

—Where from? Where the darkies beat their feet on the Mississippi mud. That where from.

—Is that from a song or something?

—That right. A song or something. Ain't no darkies in Chicago, even if the white boys still sing about them and call it jazz. You been here five days. Where was you six days ago?

—Between places, I said.

—Cheap answer. Ain't no need for it. You mysterious without it.

—Mysterious?

—Sure. You like that? Being mysterious.

—Yeah, I said. —It's grand.

—Grand.

—Yeah. How am I mysterious?

—Oh boy, she said. —We going to talk about you all the day?

—No, I said. —But give us five minutes.

—Well, she said. —I gave you two of my names. Remember them?

—Dora and Ethel.

—That right. So how come you was calling me Annie and Miss O'Shea? What shit you got going on there? You fucking your old schoolmarm last night?

—Well. Yeah, I said. —Now and again.

She didn't object.

—You Irish, right?

—Yeah.

—And your schoolmarm in Ireland a coloured woman?

—No, I said. —But she's beautiful and a woman. And it was dark.

—How come you was at that club on a Monday night?

—It was just Monday, I said.

—Notice something?

—Like what?

—Like you was just about the only ofay in the joint. Monday night is coloured night.

—Ofay?

—White.

—Oh. I noticed that, alright.

—And it not scare you?

—No.

91

—Surrounded by all those coloured women and their angry men wanting to kill you for looking at them?

—No.

—I believe you, Henry S.

—Grand.

My only real friends had been women; I could always talk to women. I missed Piano Annie. I missed old Missis O'Shea. I even missed the old witch, Granny Nash. She'd always known what I was up to; she probably still did. And, Christ, I missed Miss O'Shea. I turned every corner expecting to see her, even though there were thousands of miles between us, as far as I could know, and it was five years, more, since I'd seen her and longer still since I'd been able to hold her. I'd heard nothing of her; I didn't know if she was free or still in jail, fighting her war or rearing our growing daughter, missing me or doing what I'd been doing for years, running away.

And I wondered now if Hettie had ever found the wallet. Or if someone else had found it. If the photo was still there, waiting, with the money. Was it there? I weighed the thought. No. It was gone and spent, and thrown aside, away.

I stared at Dora. She was beautiful.

—What colour are you? I asked.

She took her hand from my back and passed it across my eyes.

—I just been fucking a blind man, she said.

—I'm serious, I said. —What colour are you?

—Well, from where you are, I'm a nigger.

—No.

—Yes. A negro, if you want. A negress. A darkie. A shine. They're all nigger. You're here because I'm a fine-looking negress. That's what you see.

—You're a fine-looking woman.

—And any woman will do if you get to call her Annie or Miss O'Shea.

Her hand was on my back again, in a circle between my shoulder blades. Round and slowly around, no push, no anger, no hard point being made. My latest teacher, presenting me with nothing but the facts.

—Now, if you was a Negro sitting there, I'd be a high-yaller bitch. I'd be one bright yellow feather in your cap, black boy.

—Why?

—Because I ain't as much of a nigger as you are, that's why. I'm the nearest thing to white you'll ever get to weigh in your hands.

—So what?

—So what? How long you been here?

—Three or four years.

—Three or four years. And you can say, So what. You *are* blind.

—I've been busy, I told her.

—Busy! she said. —Boy, you been asleep! You got no right to be here that time and not notice a thing or two. No right.

She slapped my shoulder.

—You Irish and you telling me you don't know the difference between black and white? You don't know the rules? You people wrote most of the goddam rules. What day we meet?

—Monday, I said.

—That right, she said. —Monday. Because I wouldn't be there Tuesday, Wednesday, Thursday, Friday, Saturday or Sunday. And if you say, Why not, I'll tear your balls off and throw them down to the street.

—Because you're coloured, I said.

It was feeble but the best I could manage. She was terrifying and marvellous.

—That right, she said. —I'm coloured. No coloured let in that door any other day of the week. Monday our night. Even on State Street. Our street.

—It's a shame, I said.

—A crying goddam shame, she said. —Five, six more days to Monday. What am I going to do?

—You could pass for white, I said.

—You know more than you pretend, she said. —I don't want to pass for white.

—We could always stay in, I said.

—About all we can do, she said. —'Less we want to get

93

ourselves troubled. You want to know why I ain't interested in being a white woman no more?

—Fire away, I said.

She stared at me.

—It ain't because I can never be one, she said. —That ain't it. I spent all my life being less than white. Thinking I was better than most because I had some white man's blood, and knowing all the time that I was just a nigger bitch. Get my hair straighted, put bleach on my face, I was still a nigger bitch. And not enough of a nigger neither. Not white enough, not black enough. Just a jaundice-coloured bitch, didn't matter a goddam how many men was after my tail. I hated my own self and walked through those nigger bitches thinking I was better than them because my ass wasn't as black as their black asses.

She said nothing for a while. She hummed something that I couldn't catch. Then she looked at me and spoke.

—Took a long time to get out of that white man's trap. Want to know who did it for me?

—Who?

—Dipper.

—Armstrong?

—That right.

She hummed again, and looked at me.

—Be what you be. That what he said. And that the way he plays.

She rubbed the blanket like it was a cat on her lap.

—Want to meet him?

—Yeah.

—You never know, she said. —Maybe he can cure you being Irish.

—He already has, I said.

—No, brother, she said. —Ain't that easy.

He was dressed only in big white towels, one around his waist, the other wrapped around his neck. He'd been off the stage ten minutes but the sweat was still flowing onto his neck and down his chest and arms. He wiped his forehead with the handkerchief he'd had with him onstage. Off the stage, he was a small man but his smile and his face were huge, and everything and everyone surrounded him. The dressing room was crowded with sharp-dressed white men and women, but I could see none of the other musicians.

Dora had just introduced me to him. She was white tonight – this once, for me – the only way to get us together through the big, leather-padded doors. The white boys in charge of the door knew her; they knew her when she was black too, but that didn't matter. Tonight she was white, and she was with a white man. She was inside the rules.

He was sitting deep in a broken chair, but he stood up to meet me. He stood in front of me and held out his hand. Then he saw something, and the hand went further, and gently grabbed one of my lapels. He felt its threads with the fingers that had helped him to his impossible notes – a long line of them that had sliced the roof a few minutes earlier. I could feel the heat of his fingers close to my face. He was standing right against me. I could smell his work and genius.

—That's a mighty sharp vine, Pops, he said.

More than three years after I'd bought it, the suit was still an eye-catcher; my first American suit, my own wear and tear hadn't worn down the fabric.

—It one of Mister Piper's? he asked.

—Don't know him, I said.

—Mister Scotty Piper, he said. —Fine, fine tailor.

—It's not one of his.

He looked down at the trousers.

—And the nice wide pants, he said.

—I saw them coming, I told him.

He smiled.

I was remembering how, giving it the old Henry.

—I got there before the rest, I said. —But, you know yourself, it's the shoulders. The difference between a good suit and a bad one.

—Well, that the truth, he said.

He laughed and slapped my shoulders. He looked at me carefully. Then he looked at Dora.

—He features somebody I know, he said.

95

He looked at me again. He looked up at my face.

—We met before, Pops?

—No, I said.

—No, he said. —But it's a problem. You ofays all look the same to me.

That got laughs; I didn't mind.

—An ofay that can carry a coloured suit, he said. —We got to talk, Pops.

He picked up his trousers, then turned to me again.

—Hang around.

Dora shoved me with her hip.

I was in.

It was the same night that Sacco and Vanzetti were finally strapped to the chair and cooked; I saw it on the front pages the day after. But I was happy that night. I'd been to see *The General* at the Paradise, my first film since New York. I sat through it twice, laughed twice as hard at Buster Keaton, and forgot that my girl wasn't at my side. She was sitting above me, in the gods, up in nigger heaven. She was black that afternoon. And now my hand was still wet with Louis Armstrong's sweat. He'd held my hand; he'd seen the man I used to be. A man who carried a good suit through checkpoints and locked doors. Louis Armstrong had looked at me and seen someone he wanted, a man he needed to know, a man who'd stroll right on with him. He'd seen Henry Smart.

It was months before we spoke again but it didn't matter. I waited and, sometimes, I knew.

I waited now for Dora.

Sometimes she got off her streetcar three blocks before her stop, and sometimes she didn't. She sat in the car and looked ahead or down at her book as I stood and watched her pass. She looked older, coming home from work. And, sometimes, maybe once a week, she stepped off and there I was, sometimes. Sometimes, she went straight past me and, sometimes, I jumped on the car and left her there.

She was white enough to work in the Loop but she'd given that up. She worked for a family now, in Oak Park.

—Clean some, cook some. Do what the bitch should do her

own self.

Doing the black woman's work. It paid less than the Loop dress shop had, and the hours were longer, but she wasn't pretending now. No more hair straighteners or powders, no more care with the accent.

—Don't play it up neither. I just be Dora.

—So you're happier.

—Don't be so dumb, Henry S.

I took care; I even noticed – but I still didn't get it. I'd spent three years trying not to be Irish, but I didn't understand. I thought I did, but I was never close enough.

—You think they live here cos they want to? she asked me once, when she met me off the trolley, before she got too angry to talk to me. —There's a line, Henry S., and you don't see it cos you don't have to. But we do.

—I only said I liked it, I told her.

But she'd gone. I watched her stride away, under a string of rabbits that hung from a telegraph pole, across the pavement, to a window above a butcher's door. Her anger made the rabbits swing. The red in her head-rag caught the yellow streetlight, threw it back.

That was all I'd said: I liked the place. I saw the alleys. I saw the kids – the rickets and glaucoma. I saw what the houses were, the old rotten homes of the rich, worse, more packed, than the one I slept in; as bad, sometimes, as the one I'd been born in. And I'd seen few black men working in the packing houses. And fewer in the push of men at the gates every morning, hoping for their turn and the nod. And none in the Loop going in and out the front doors, none that weren't moving off the streets, getting quickly to where they were going.

I wasn't a sap.

—I only said I liked it here.

I ran after her.

—You fuckin' like it.

—Go away, fool.

But I kept up, got beside her, made men and women step out of our way.

—What you doing?

It wasn't fair; I knew that. I was drawing attention, dragging it to her, just to prove her wrong. To prove that we could stand here and talk, that we could do it as long as we wanted.

Past the Palace-de-Luxe Beauty Shop, and no one in the window took much notice. I looked back, and I was right – three lye-soaked heads waiting for the next sight to see – we were already gone. The loan bank, the bargain store, the storefront church – no hard eyes or mutters. Past the poolroom and barber shop and the hard men who always stood outside. They stared, more frankly than white men ever did, but it wasn't me they were looking at. They were gawking at a good-looking woman.

The Stroll was lighting up.

—You wait, she said.

I wasn't getting in. If she brought a white man home, she was working – she told me this. If she brought him home more than twice, or he started arriving by himself, using what looked like his own key, started nodding at folks, patting the heads of kids on the steps – the stoop, she was attracting bad attention. I hadn't been back to her room. And the room wasn't hers. She shared the rent with four other girls. They'd been on a round-trip excursion to Memphis the first night she'd parked herself in front of me. They left on Friday night, got back on Monday morning, partied all the way and back—

—A dance on wheels, she said.

—Ever do it yourself?

—No reason to, she said.

—back in time for the charge to work. But they'd missed the train, all four of them, and rolled back into town a whole week late.

While she changed, took off the servant's head-rag and threw it in a corner with the years she didn't want, I waited on the corner of 35th and State, the district's big corner, and listened to a tailgate band, on the back of a flatbed truck parked right against the pavement. There was a piano player

I'd seen and heard before. Albert Ammons. He was up there with a trombone player and a drummer, and a guitarist, sharing the stool with Mister Ammons, all on the back of the truck, under a banner advertising the same trip that had sent Dora's flat-mates south, the Illinois Central round-trip excursion to Memphis. There was a barker too, in a sharp suit and polished derby, sitting on the fireplug, waving tickets, and often selling, to anyone who stopped to hear the band.

—I got them here, folks! Got them right here!

He stayed away from me.

—Tickets here to Paradise! All way home to the land of cotton *and* change in your pocket!

It was good music. Men grabbed home-bound women, made a dance floor right outside the loan bank.

—If you can't do it a long time, do it twice!

It was the rough sound of home, played for city floors and pavements; it was good-time music for homesick slickers.

—Oh, shake your wicked knees!

There were four couples dancing now, flinging and flung, moving just enough, watched and clapped by dozens more, six or seven couples now, and Mister Ammons thumping out the steps and shouting as the barker shouted. This was what I'd meant; this was what I liked. The back-home music of Manhattan's Lower East Side had been miserable; even the reels were meant to draw the tears. But these men here were beating out the blues, and laughing as they worked. The steps hadn't come north with the dancers; they were made up, there, on the sidewalk, and abandoned when the barker decided that enough was enough. There was no one left buying. They could come back in an hour, the next day, next week, and the steps would be brand-new different.

The dancers sensed it, knew it in the shift in tempo.

—Oh, shake, shake, shake your fat fanny!

Their dance was nearly over. The guitar man climbed over the side of the truck, and the dancers turned and grabbed each other; they left the ground, inches below, a whirr of hats and elbows. The streetlight couldn't hold them clear.

Oh, play that thing.

The barker had the last word before he hopped onto the running board.

—These fine, high-powered maestros be playing their fine, high-powered stomps and boogie-blues, in the fine, high-powered choo-choo train, all the way to Memphis, Tennessee. The Shimmy, the Black Bottom, the Charleston. All can be dooed in the Coloured Only car. All night, all the way. Every number a gassuh.

The trombone player jumped from the back of the truck, holding the instrument high. He waved back, and walked away. The truck moved out in the opposite direction, to join the State Street crawl. Mister Ammons was still belting away, although the other men held onto the sides of the truck. And, as they crept over the intersection and moved more freely south, his piano was joined and swallowed by other pianos and horns and drums that took over the street, the streets, same time, every night.

Oh, play that thing.

This was living like I'd never seen it. This wasn't drowning the sorrow, the great escape, happy or unhappy. It was life itself, the thing and the point of it. No excuses: it was why these men and women lived.

Dora took her time, but standing on that corner was a very good night out. I soaked in the sounds, the victory and joy. The packing house was far away. I wasn't going to stay there. The pay was bad, the work was bad, and they'd be getting worse as autumn – *fall* – surrendered to my first Chicago winter. I'd had enough of Packingtown. I hadn't moved west to live with Lithuanians and Poles. They were grand, but impenetrable. Big decent, grunting people. They ate too much, too fast; they prayed too much, too often – they were too like the fuckin' Irish. I was safe there, but that was all.

I'd be safe here too, but alive again. I didn't know what I'd do, but I knew I'd be doing it here. I didn't know why – it was stupid, sentimental; I could see that. And dangerous. But not tonight, it wasn't. I was ready again, excited. I believed.

Her hand was on my arm, fingers quickly tucked in to my chest.

Her anger had been thrown in the corner, gone the way of her head-rag. She was glowing, happy, younger than she was, already dancing to the tunes and steps that were fighting it out around us. It was officially night time now, play time, and we could be together. We'd be looked at. She was gorgeous and I wasn't far off it. Henry Smart again, because she'd looked at me. I'd come out of hiding. And here was a woman who'd got there before me; she'd stopped hiding too.

—We were made for each other, I said.

—No, she said. —We were not.

—Where'll we go?

—Well, now, she said. —You a white man on a coloured street that ain't your street. That the problem? No, sir. A coloured lady on her own coloured street. She the problem.

She moved, and took me with her.

—But tonight, Henry S., we got the answer to that problem.

Through men on their way home, and women on their way out, past pimps and preachers, a one-legged man with a begging cup – war or stockyards, I couldn't tell; past two black cops – I hadn't seen black cops before. We passed restaurants, cabarets, and loud speakeasies. We passed because we couldn't go there. She could enter some, or I could. But we couldn't enter together.

We strolled at a clip; she knew where we were going. They were all there, on or just off State Street: the Dreamland, the Sunset, the Plantation, the Elite Café, the De Luxe. All fighting, grabbing as we passed. But they weren't for us tonight.

We stopped a block short of the Panama Café. She let go of my arm. I knew the trick by now.

We could walk into the Panama Café.

The words had made me jump when she'd first whispered them. I went for the gun I didn't have.

—A black and what?

—Tan.

—Black and Tan?

—Yes, Henry S. What the matter?

—What the fuck is a black and tan?

—Where your blood go, Henry? You gone all pale.

I told her all about the Black and Tans. (The headlights caught the corners of our eyes, then sprayed across our shoulders and made black shadows of the way ahead. We heard the boot nails scratch wood as the Tans abandoned the tenders to chase us. They were right behind us now. We could feel their pace in the ground. They were fit, angry men, an army of them on our backs.)

OUR HIDDEN LIVES

BY SIMON GARFIELD

In 1936, the anthropologist Tom Harrisson arrived back in England from the South Pacific, where he had been studying cannibals. Within weeks of his return he had arrived at a startling realisation: remote tribes were all very interesting, but they were not more interesting than the inhabitants of Bolton, where Harrisson lived. What was needed, he believed, was an 'anthropology of ourselves', a study of everyday people living regular lives. He reasoned that the press was not providing this service, and the government did not understand the most basic attitudes, desires and fears of those they served.

He was not alone in these opinions. With two colleagues he placed notices in newspapers and magazines asking for volunteers willing to share the frank details of their everyday lives. More than 1,000 responded, many agreeing to keep daily diaries.

Most had stopped writing by 1945, but a few carried on as the country emerged to face momentous change and great challenges. *Our Hidden Lives* features the edited highlights of five of these diarists, and is, I hope, an invaluable record of one of the most under-examined periods in our recent past. The writing is sometimes despairing, often moving, occasionally bitter, frequently prescient, and occasionally just plain funny. There is Edie Rutherford, 43 at the end of the war, a proud and sometimes sanctimonious housewife in Sheffield, married to a timber merchant and football fanatic, dismayed at the price of cod, delighted with the Labour government despite everything.

There is George Taylor, an accountant in his mid-forties, also living in Sheffield, a keen supporter of Esperanto and the Workers' Educational Association, unable to resist a cheap offer of linoleum, forever trying to finish a novel he began reading 13 years earlier.

There is Maggie Joy Blunt, a lyrical and talented writer in her mid-thirties living in a cottage near Slough, forced by circumstance to take in lodgers, ever hunting down new supplies of cigarettes, once again failing in her ambition to have an early night.

There is Herbert Brush, 72, a widowed retired electrical engineer living in south east London, spending much time tending celeriac on his allotment, frequently ambushed by the local gossip, writing copious amounts of poetry about the fuel crisis, the fate of Hitler and his own mortality.

And then there is B Charles, a gay antiques dealer and tutor in his mid-fifties, once of Windsor but now of Edinburgh, previously a dresser in the theatre, a man not delighted by Hollywood films or other trappings of the modern world, still bitter over the mysterious details of his father's will, a regular prowler around the local bars in search of younger men who may benefit from his unusual course in 'personality development'. Mr Charles only began writing in November 1945, and so there are no entries from him in the following extract (you'll just have to buy the book!)

Occasionally the diarists questioned the value of what they were doing, wondering whether anyone would be interested in their observations in years to come. They needn't have worried: their writing is unique, and the most illuminating record of an astonishing time.

Simon Garfield

£19.99
ISBN: 0091896959
Published September 2004

OUR TROUBLES ARE ONLY JUST BEGINNING

TUESDAY, 1 MAY 1945

Maggie Joy Blunt
Freelance writer and publicity officer in metal factory, living in Burnham Beeches, near Slough
Important hours, important as those days at the end of August in 1939 preceding the declaration of war. This is tension of a different kind, expectancy, preparations being made for a change in our way of living. But the tempo is slower. We wait, without anxiety, for the official announcement by Mr Churchill that is to herald two full days' holiday and the beginning of another period of peace in Europe. We wait wondering if Hitler is dying or dead or will commit suicide or be captured and tried and shot, and what his henchman are doing and feeling.

All the women of my acquaintance have strongly disapproved today of the treatment of the bodies of Mussolini and his mistress. I heard one man in the sales department when he was told that the bodies had been hung up by the feet say glibly 'Good thing too!' But RW and myself and Lys and Miss M are shocked and disgusted. Spitting on the bodies, shooting at them, seems childish and barbarous, and such actions cannot bring the dead to life or repair damage and is a poor sort of vengeance. What a state the world is in and what a poor outlook for the future.

I have worn myself out spring cleaning the sitting room. All

Sunday and yesterday at it – it now looks so brilliant and beautiful I'll never dare live in it.

We had ice cream in canteen for lunch today – the first for two or is it three years?

George Taylor
Accountant in Sheffield
I noticed that the flags which were flying on the Town Hall yesterday, presumably in preparation for peace, have been taken down. Apparently the officials were premature in their preparations.

WEDNESDAY, 2 MAY

Maggie Joy Blunt
One can hardly keep pace with the news. 'Hitler Dead' the *News Chronicle* informed me this morning in 12-inch type across the front page. Doenitz has either been appointed to succeed him or has seized power over Himmler's head . . . We discussed the situation all through lunch, wondering how much longer the war would now continue with Doenitz in control. At the office an atmosphere of suspense but little obvious excitement.

George Taylor
News of Hitler's death has caused little stir. I never heard it mentioned on my tram journeys to and from work, none of the clients I met breathed his name, and the only person who mentioned him to me was my thirty-two-year-old colleague. He doubted very much his death, but I said that in my opinion he was indeed dead, but that he had died from natural causes and not in the fighting.

I was completely surprised at 9.10 a.m. to hear of the surrender of the German forces in Italy. It has been a well-kept secret, and I should have been less surprised by a surrender in the West. Events are certainly moving now.

Herbert Brush
Retired electrical engineer, south-east London
Good news. Hitler is really dead. I wonder what sort of
reception his astral form has received on the other side.

> I can imagine when he came
> And when his victims heard his name
> They gathered round him not to miss
> So good a chance to hoot and hiss
>
> But those on earth may all agree
> From torture he must not go free
> That God Almighty has some plan
> To punish such a naughty man

THURSDAY, 3 MAY

George Taylor
Now that there seems every prospect of VE day being
celebrated in the near future, my audit assistant, a married
woman of twenty-five, seems mostly interested in when we
are to have the holiday. Her forecast is Saturday lunchtime,
with the rest of the day holiday and VE plus one will be
Sunday. I suppose that is ingrained pessimism.

Police duty on a wretchedly cold and rainy evening. During
the patrol my sergeant was telling me of the arrangements to
celebrate in the works. It seems that some are to pay time-and-
a-half for the hours worked between the signal and closing
down on VE day, and full time for the following two days.
Another works has set aside £3 for all employees as pay for
the three days. In his own office, a Friendly Society, the girls
were asking about the holiday, and when he said that they
would be working as usual unless they received specific
instructions to the contrary, they were loud in protest. One,
indeed, declared flatly that she would not turn in.

Herbert Brush
The news is good this morning. I am wondering now whether

Hitler died from a clot on his brain, whether he was murdered, or whether he shot himself or took poison. I suppose that the details will come out in due course, unless they have had his body cremated.

They probably want his name to become a legend, something like our King Arthur, so that the young Germans in the twenty-first can be told what a wonderful person Hitler was, and how he died a warrior's death while fighting for his country against enormous odds.

I don't like the idea that we have to feed all the millions of prisoners taken. Most of them are young Nazis who never will be any good in the world now, after they were brought up. I am still of the opinion that all those under twenty-five should go into a lethal chamber, for the future peace of the world. It rained most of the night.

FRIDAY, 4 MAY

Herbert Brush
The trams are not running today owing to a strike. I guess there will be a lot of this kind of trouble when 'Peace' comes.

Maggie Joy Blunt
When the first newsflash came through the radio announcing the surrender of the German forces in north-west Germany, I was in bed mopping my ears. We had looked at the headlines in the *Evening News* in the office just before 5 p.m. and decided that the end must be near now, as the enemy was collapsing on all fronts.

I asked RW what she intended to do on VE day and she said that she didn't know. Her people keep a pub in Windsor and they have not decided whether they will keep open or not. If they do (and the brewers want them to) they will not have more than their normal rationed supply and will be sold out by 9.30 p.m. Her father thinks he will invite in all his pals and keep the pub closed to the public.

No one seems very certain what they will do. There are to be some Victory parades and special services and bonfires. It looks as though I shall spend the day and days following in close, solitary seclusion. My ears are a most revolting sight and even Dr B is baffled. He talks of sending me to a specialist but I am to treat them myself this weekend with rainwater and special ointment. I am worried and tired and do not want to go out or meet anyone. I have been going to the office every day this week after a visit to the doctor in the morning and coming home early. My friends are sympathetic and anxious but I feel rather a leper and imagine all strangers to be goggling at me.

I came home at 5 p.m., collected ointment from the chemist, and, while waiting for it to be made up, some new stock arrived including a small box of Wright's coal tar soap. I have not seen any of this for a long while and the girls said they would not have any 'for ages' so I bought two tablets. I bought lettuce, radishes, beetroot and mustard and cress, came home, prepared salad, Hovis and butter, glass of milk, honey and an orange, and got into bed and ate it there. Since when I have been dealing with the ears and listening to the news.

Girls in cloakroom were chattering excitedly this afternoon. 'Oh, I do hope it'll happen while we're at work! – It won't seem the same will it?' The official notice asks us all to assemble in the canteen where news of victory is announced over the works broadcasting system. We are then to have the rest of the day off and the two following days. The girls began twittering about their husbands – what group for demobilisation did each belong to? I left them, feeling rather old and forlorn.

Listening now to the repeat broadcast of General Montgomery from Germany this afternoon. My emotions at this moment are indescribable: enormous pride in the fact that I am British, wonder and excitement. 'Tomorrow morning at 8 a.m. the war in Europe will be over . . .' The war in Europe is over . . . This is a tremendous moment.

The war is over. I cry a little. I think of my dearest friends, my stepmother, my brother in Egypt, of those men in the fighting services I have known – and I wish I had taken a more active part; it is too late now. But it is not too late to take part in the new fight ahead. I am not moved to rush out tomorrow and wave a Union Jack in the village high street. I think it is a good sign that people are saying universally 'Our troubles are only just beginning', because it would be idiotic to assume they are over with the end of hostilities.

We want a better world and we must fight for it. That is where we must distinguish between pessimism and optimism. I believe with the utmost optimism, faith, hope and joy that we can have our better world (and note that one says 'a better world' – not the perfect or even best possible world) – yes, that we can have it if we know clearly what we want and fight for it.

Midnight news now being read. The announcer sounds tired. Pockets of German resistance still remain. I have been down and turned off the radio. For once I waited to hear the whole of the National Anthem, moved suddenly again to tears by this historic, this incredible moment. I stood with my hand on the radio switch listening to the National Anthem and to the voices of a thousand, thousand ghosts. They came over the air into that unlit, silent room, I swear it.

It's time I tried to sleep. One of the cats is outside my window waiting to be let in. Tomorrow and tomorrow and tomorrow stretch before me. Infinitely more full of promise and interest than the war years have been. I feel that new and exciting events await me. But that may be due to the influence of tonight's news. The atmosphere is charged with a release and potentiality.

And the bottom sheet, in an exceedingly frail condition from old age and much hard wear, is now torn beyond hope and redemption. I am sick to death of patching worn linen.

George Taylor

The monthly executive committee meeting of the Workers' Educational Association. As an experiment next year we are having a class on Appreciation of the Films, and a most attractive syllabus has been drawn up. The committee members are a little afraid, however, that the class may be used for entertainment purposes only, and they have fixed a class fee of 10/- to emphasise that serious study is intended.

SATURDAY, 5 MAY

Maggie Joy Blunt
Awakened this morning by neighbour Mrs C shouting something to the butcher. Don't know yet what he has left me – in saucepan in shed outside my backdoor. It has been pouring with rain from the time I woke and I am spending the morning in bed, reading the papers which repeat last night's broadcast news, attending to the ears which do seem a little better, and dozing. Have cancelled a hair appointment, intend to have an early (salad) lunch and then get up. Shall light kitchen fire, tidy the kitchen, go into the village, return to kitchen tea, maybe have the kittens down, wash a very large collection of soiled 'smalls' and look out for material for making two new cushioned squares for the sitting room – that is my programme. Why do people 'wonder what I do with myself all alone'?

The radio has been on and will be while I am indoors lest I miss some important gobbet of information. One of the dangers I think of having the news brought to one so quickly when history is being as dramatic as it is at present is that it makes one want and expect life to move with the speed of a film towards some happy conclusion.

Herbert Brush
W and I went to the Capitol Cinema this afternoon. The German prison camp was shown: it was not very clear, but clear enough to make me want to put our Nazi prisoners in under the same conditions. Nothing less will make those sub-human beasts realise that it is wrong to torture other folk in such cruel ways. Even the women guards must have been sadists of the worst type, who enjoyed seeing and making their victims suffer. Judging by the short glimpse I had of these females' faces, I could easily imagine them singing and cursing as they beat their helpless prisoners.

111

One of the films was awful piffle, but the other with Wallace Beery in it was good.

SUNDAY, 6 MAY

Maggie Joy Blunt
The end of hostilities in Europe is to be announced within the next day or two, we are told, and before Thursday when Mr Churchill is making a special broadcast.

Lys came to tea and stayed the evening. Her friend C called in about 6.30. She left a spare pint of milk for us, two eggs for Lys and some ointment for my ears, which has, so she assures me, positively magic powers and has been used by people of her acquaintance who have had the same trouble and found it effective where other remedies have failed. We had a drink and wondered when the announcement would be. Lys thinks she will go home that day and read a good book. C, whose husband is in the forces and stationed nearby, expects to hear from him and have him home for two days.

I have, urged on by Lys, answered an ad in this week's *New Statesman* for a job in a publishing firm. Not that I expect any results but it is good for one's morale to make this kind of effort when one feels in a rut as I do.

MONDAY, 7 MAY

George Taylor
No news of VE day, so to the office as usual, and my wife went collecting rents. When I arrived back at the office after lunch, my thirty-two-year-old colleague said that his assistant, seventeen, had overheard a prominent solicitor say that peace would be announced at 4 p.m. Another person he had met, who was 'in the know', also gave the same time. A few minutes later I went out, and overheard a tram conductress say to her mate, 'Well, the war will be over at 4 p.m.' We did not settle down to any serious work at the office, and listened for the church bells at 4 p.m., but they did not come, so we lingered on till 5.30. Meanwhile, the office boy had

brought in an evening paper which announced that VE day would be tomorrow.

Town was very busy, and there was a holiday atmosphere everywhere. It took me nearly a quarter of an hour longer than usual to get home, so I just missed the 6 p.m. news. However, my wife said there was nothing in it, so we did not know what to think. Hoping to see a news film we went to the local cinema, but they did not show even a newsflash, the whole time being taken up with *The Adventures of Mark Twain*. We were thoroughly disgusted.

Maggie Joy Blunt

Had a £1 note taken from my handbag at work this week. Like most women there I leave it about unguarded – we do not suspect each other of petty theft. Other people have been missing notes recently also and when I reported my loss to the works police I was told that they had their eye on a certain office boy. I hate everything of this kind happening and won't – I can't – accuse anyone, but I believe I know the boy they mean. He is a weasely looking lad, impertinent and difficult to handle, but responds I find to a touch of humour – scolding only makes him sullen and disobedient. No doubt he thinks me a good-natured mug. My feelings about him are that he is a slippery, sharp, incurable type, always quite well dressed as though from a fairly good home, but there is something about him, some destiny in his face and manner. No remand home or schooling will make any difference. He won't listen. He will just follow the force that is urging him along a certain path.

From Italy, S wrote on 1 May:

Last night German resistance on the northern Italian front ended. I was at my desk with two very young officers and my OC who was a captain with me in Greece in 1941. He said, 'It's been a long road.' We opened a bottle of Scotch and had a lot. Yet the old real Desert Rats – my old 7th Armoured Division – are still battling around Hamburg. The youngsters felt more exhilaration than we. My thoughts, strangely, were on the safari track from Bug Bug to Maddelena – two graves long since covered with sand. The end is near now and a great sense of emptiness. A new desert of emotion to be explored and fought over . . .

Herbert Brush
I went to the Royal Academy exhibition in Piccadilly. My word, it was hot walking in the sun, and by the time I arrived there perspiration was standing on my forehead. The show cost a shilling. I put a pencil mark in the catalogue against the exhibits that were able to keep me in front of them for more than five seconds.

No. 31: *Girl Resting* by A. R. Middleton. She is naked, but it was the position of her left foot that caught my eye and I wondered how she could pose in that position without getting cramp.

No. 88: *Snow in Nottinghamshire* by Henry Moore. The reason I looked at this is because there are hills and valleys in the background, and I could not remember if there are hills in Notts.

No. 184: *Still Life* by Frederick Elwell. There is a cold ham with a nice wide cut in the middle showing the inside lean part, and a pork pie with a couple of bottles of spirit alongside. It made me feel hungry, and I remembered that I had a sausage roll in my pocket, but I could not eat a sausage roll in the Royal Academy.

I left the exhibition at 2.45 p.m. I walked as far as the Haymarket and caught a No.12 bus. A crowd was waiting at the end of Downing Street, presumably waiting to see the Prime Minister, who is expected to declare Peace today.

TUESDAY, 8 MAY

George Taylor
There was the stillness of a Sunday when we woke, and this continued all morning. I spent the morning doing some useful work in the garden, and then, as it started to rain, stayed in

during the afternoon. Although we knew what Churchill was going to say at 3 p.m. – or at least what we hoped he would say – we switched on the radio and continued listening until nearly 5 p.m.

After tea we went for a short walk and found quite a few flags displayed by the houses, although there was nothing elaborate. From the look of the trams we thought there could have been very few in town this afternoon, but a friend we met told us that there had been thousands. We still cannot realise that the war in Europe is indeed at an end. It is true that I have removed some more of the blackout today, as I promised myself on Peace Day, but somehow I still have a sneaking feeling that it may be wanted again any time.

In January 1941 we purchased some tinned chicken, and as we have never been called upon to use it, we promised ourselves a treat on Peace Day, and we did open it today. As with many things, it proved somewhat of a disappointment, for although it is genuine chicken – bones, skin and meat – it is spoilt by aspic jelly. Another long cherished tin, of sausages purchased in November 1940, proved much more acceptable for lunch.

Herbert Brush
I wonder whether any two of the millions of people in London will think the same thoughts today about the date when the change in their lives from War to Peace commenced.

I heard Mr Churchill at 3 p.m. declare that war will end at 12.01 tonight. I wonder why the extra minute was added? Then an account of the various crowds collected in London and elsewhere, which made me glad that I was not in one of them.

I nearly swore this afternoon when I found that nearly all my runner beans had been eaten before they put their tips above the ground. I shall have to sow them all afresh: luckily I have plenty of my own seed.

WEDNESDAY, 9 MAY

George Taylor
Finished taking down blackouts at all windows and fanlights,

and parcelled them for storage in the loft, ready for the next war. If we do leave this house before then, they will go along with the fixtures. I hope, however, that we shall be able to forget their existence. Bank holiday crowds everywhere.

Herbert Brush
7 p.m. I have been on the plot most of the day. I believe the judges in the competition come round for their first visit before the middle of May, so I have been busy trying to make the plot tidy. I have fixed up another seat at the end of plot close to the hedge so that I can sit in the shelter during showers. This was the spot where I pressed myself into the hedge with the bucket over my head when a rocket burst overhead and bits of it came down all round me.

FRIDAY, 11 MAY

Edie Rutherford
Housewife and clerk in Sheffield
Where to begin? Well, we came home from work on Monday evening, 'bewitched, buggered and bewildered' as a friend of ours used to say. We had our office wireless on hourly without getting any satisfaction.

Then at 9 p.m. we got the news that the next two days were holidays. That was enough for me. The following day I had promised to go to help my friend who is still clearing up her house, so husband came with me. I had stood in a queue for two small brown loaves for them. There were bread and fish queues everywhere all along the bus route and our tram route to town.

A neighbour brought in her portable radio at 3 p.m. so that we could listen to Churchill. He spoke well and seemed in good form. Everyone agreed that we have been well blessed in having such a leader. I felt once again great gratitude for being born British.

Left at 5 p.m. and walked to nearest tram so that we could come home via town centre. Thousands round City Hall for a service. More thousands just wandering about. All the little mean streets had their decorations just as for Coronation and Jubilee. I find them pathetic though courageous.

We got home and had a meal and sat quietly till 10 p.m. when we decided to go and have a look round. These flats had a neon 'V' right on the top flat roof which looked effective. Also our corridor balcony lights were on for the first time since blackout began. At the street corner, our shopping district, a radio shop had fitted up loudspeakers and music blared out. We saw many people the worse for drink, in fact most that we saw were in that state. Either looking very sorry for themselves or just merry, and we also saw vomit about, ugh.

Met up with a spinster who lives alone on this floor who asked could she stroll with us so of course we said she could. Came home about 11 p.m., decided we were hungry and what about looking at reserve food put by years ago. To our surprise and pleasure found a tin of asparagus tips and tin of tomatoes. Had these with cheese and water biscuits and margarine. Miss S found a stout for husband at her flat and one gin and ginger for herself and myself. Then we sat and talked till 1.20.

Went to door to see friend off and found terrace floodlit and loudspeakers giving music for tenants and their friends to dance, and they all seemed merry. Kept it up till 2 a.m. when, I heard since, someone on a higher floor threw water over them.

I thought, as always, that the King's speech was marred by his speech, but on the whole his stammer wasn't so bad. Maybe if he were to speak to us more often he would learn to relax so well that he would not stammer at all. I have decided these last few days that 'Rule, Britannia!' is a far better tune than 'God Save The King'.

Weather forecasts are a welcome return and we don't care how many deep depressions threaten from Iceland or anywhere. We can bear that kind of depression now. Anyone want tin hats and two gas masks?

George Taylor
I was alone for lunch at home, and noticed there was a symphony on the radio, so switched on for company. It was

Beethoven's Fifth. Some fortnight ago I had booked for the Hallé concert in the evening tonight, and to refresh my memory as to the programme I turned up the advertisement in the daily paper. Lo and behold, the programme had been altered, and Beethoven's Fifth Symphony included there. Twice hearing in one day is pretty good going.

At the Hallé concert there was a very thin attendance, the poorest I have seen for some time. To start, we had three national anthems, I presume the American and Russian played in full, then the British. When we sat down my neighbour remarked, 'It's a good job they didn't play the Chinese.'

TUESDAY, 15 MAY

Edie Rutherford
Yesterday I had a cable from my goddaughter in Natal – rejoicing about our victory and assuring me I am in their thoughts at this time. Kind gesture.

Friend tells me that he gave a talk to Jewish Youth at a club in town one night last week and was amazed at the intelligent questions afterwards. I listened and told him that in my opinion the Jews need to sort out their own minds, i.e. they want Socialism because they believe it makes no distinction of class, colour or creed; yet they want capitalism because so many of them are capitalist.

Shops now display notices that they have plenty of torch batteries . . . GOD BLESS OUR LADS FOR THIS VICTORY is painted on sides of houses near where I work. Others thank Monty, Churchill, Roosevelt, Stalin. Clear that decorations were planned some time ago as all show Roosevelt; or is it that folk feel he should get the credit?

Churchill sounded tired when he spoke on Sunday. I think he should be put to grass, as he calls it. Can't understand why he doesn't admit it and be done with it.

1/- for a small lettuce . . . oh well. No cress about just now. There are suggestions that we are going to be worse off than ever for food. I believe I would not mind that if the variety could be improved. My husband is quite definitely suffering from poor nutrition today. He needs more milk, butter, cream . . . I'm terribly worried about him.

WEDNESDAY, 16 MAY

George Taylor
The news of the restoration of the basic petrol ration has brought no joy to me. One of the great blessings of the war has been the reduction of motor traffic on the roads, and I dread seeing all the private cars back again. I think that peacetime public transport services should have been restored before private motoring was let loose on us again.

Gardening and typing in the evening. I also listened to the BBC broadcast 'Tribute to the RAF'. It was good to hear one of these feature programmes not messed up with incidental music.

SATURDAY, 19 MAY

Herbert Brush
Roger the dog did not give any trouble during the night but he is now wandering about the house like a lost dog. Went to the Duchess Theatre to see a play by Noël Coward, *Blithe Spirit*, a weird fantasy in which the spirit of a dead wife made things uncomfortable for a man who had married again. Irene Browne was good in her part as a medium. It is some years since I went to the theatre, and I am not sure what I prefer – theatre or cinema.

SUNDAY, 20 MAY

Edie Rutherford
I just haven't had a chance to see to this diary. On Friday husband woke with temperature so I bullied him into staying in bed, rang his brother and took the opportunity to tell him how worried I am about Sid these days, and that I won't be satisfied till he has been screened; also said Sid should have

119

two weeks' holiday this year as he needs it. Harold says he would mention the screening to Sid, and see that he gets the latter. So I hope I have achieved something. One has to go about things so carefully.

WHIT MONDAY, 21 MAY

Maggie Joy Blunt
At rest now, in the domestic respectability and peace of a suburban garden. Warm sun, large clouds, cool wind, neighbours' voices, one or two aeroplanes, birds full-throated, joyous.

Saturday morning I went to have hair done in Windsor, did some shopping, had lunch, came home, cycled into village to order rations, take shoes to be mended, collect some paraffin oil in bottles. Collecting milk from next door, Lady A bears down on me with a triumphant, exultant gleam in her eye: 'I have always said that our troubles would begin when the war was over – now everyone is out for himself and there is a clash of interests everywhere. Power goes to heads of these people who have not been brought up to rule . . .' I agree that the future promises to be chaotic and that there will be trouble with Russia but can't believe it will be as black as she seems to think. I go in, have tea, do some chores and cooking and start preparing myself for CL's party.

I leave – suitably clad over afternoon party frock and taking one of my few remaining pairs of real silk stocking and shoes to change into – on cycle for Windsor about 8 p.m. and arrive just before 9 p.m. Fully intended to cycle home after the party but a friend CL was expecting couldn't come so she has a spare bed and insists that I stay. A pleasant gathering. Rep theatre people, one or two Service men, a couple of Canadian RAF, a woman I recognise as having lectured a Red Cross unit on gas two years ago. We sit and talk, drinking orange gin, champagne cider or cider cup and eating delectable snacks prepared by CL. They roll back the carpet and we dance but not for long, as there isn't much room and people evidently prefer to talk.

Spent the weekend with stepmother Ella (Aunt Aggie also there). Listening to the report of Ellen Wilkinson's speech on the one o'clock news I was suddenly struck by the thought of how extraordinary it was that the BBC should allow Labour propaganda such prominence. At her statement that the Conservative Party had carried out very few reforms during their long term of office I heard Aunt Aggie snort and wondered how I could defend that view. When I am with Conservatives I find myself agreeing with Conservative opinion, when with Liberals with Liberal, Labour with Labour, Communist with Communist. It is all very confusing. Conscience and the fact that my politically-minded friends will expect me to, will probably make me vote Labour. (The election may be held, we are told now, in July, which seems too soon, too much of a rush. But why should we have to put up with the present Government until the war with Japan is over?)

N thinks we have not heard the last of the Nazis – their apparent collapse has been too quick and easy. She is not alone in this opinion. Note a new film released and reviewed this week: *The Master Race*.

10 p.m. A pleasant, lazy day. Have done nothing but sit and knit, listen to gossip and be fed excellently at regular intervals. My dear relatives. They were up I think about 7.30–8 a.m., brought me my breakfast about 9 a.m. Spent the morning washing (an electric washing machine simplifies this for them) – Aunt Aggie dealing with the clothes, Ella hanging them in the garden. Then I borrowed the iron and mended two tears in my mackintosh with Mend-a-Tear, dried up the lunch crockery which Ella was washing, sat in the garden while Ella hoed the garden path and clouds gathered like mountains. A gin and lime, supper (herrings in tomato sauce, salad, stewed gooseberries from the garden and blancmange). Rain began to fall.

SKINNY DIP

BY CARL HIAASEN

His unique blend of black comedy, and quirky characters set against a Floridian socio-political backdrop, has made Hiaasen one of the most successful of contemporary crime writers, not just in America, but worldwide. Internationally, he's a household name, which is quite an achievement given that even his website carries a pronunciation guide (Hiyasun, in case you're not sure!). He's the author of ten previous crime novels; *Hoot*, a novel for children; and three non-fiction titles: *Team Rodent: How Disney Devours The World*, and a pair of volumes of selections from his Miami Herald columns: *Kick Ass* and *Paradise Screwed*.

It's as a humorous crime novelist with a social conscience that Hiaasen has earned his reputation. He's laugh-out-loud funny, yet his comedy embraces serious subjects. He takes the social concerns that plagued other Floridian crime writers (John D. MacDonald, most notably), and weaves intricate and hilarious plots around them. Political shenanigans often play a significant role in his books. In *Skinny Dip*, it's the destruction of the Everglades that is the lynchpin of the novel.

Charles Perrone is an eco-friendly, highly-paid biologist working in the Everglades. It's unfathomable that he should flip his wife over the railings of a cruise liner. Not on their anniversary. But that's what he does. And when the investigation into her disappearance ensues, he finds out that the world is a different place without Joey. What he doesn't know is that left to die in the dark Atlantic, Joey beat the odds and with some help from a floating bail of Jamaican grass, managed to survive in the water long enough to get rescued. But she's decided to stay dead until, with the help of her rescuer, Mick Stranahan, she gets her revenge.

Skinny Dip is a novel by a fine writer at his very finest – time to try him if you haven't before.

**Recommended by Allan Buchan,
Waterstone's Prince's Street Edinburgh**

£12.99
ISBN: 0593053737
Published October 2004

At the stroke of eleven on a cool April night, a woman named Joey Perrone went overboard from a luxury deck of the cruise liner M.V. *Sun Duchess*. Plunging toward the dark Atlantic, Joey was too dumb-founded to panic.

I married an asshole, she thought, knifing headfirst into the waves.

The impact tore off her silk skirt, blouse, panties, wrist-watch and sandals, but Joey remained conscious and alert. Of course she did. She had been co-captain of her college swim team, a biographical nugget that her husband obviously had forgotten.

Bobbing in its fizzy wake, Joey watched the gaily lit *Sun Duchess* continue steaming away at twenty nautical miles per hour. Evidently only one of the other 2,049 passengers was aware of what had happened, and he wasn't telling anybody.

Bastard, Joey thought.

She noticed that her bra was down around her waist, and she wriggled free of it. To the west, under a canopy of soft amber light, the coast of Florida was visible. Joey began to swim.

The water of the Gulf Stream was slightly warmer than the air, but a brisk northeasterly wind had kicked up a messy and uncomfortable chop. Joey paced herself. To keep her mind off sharks, she replayed the noteworthy events of the week-long cruise, which had begun almost as unpromisingly as it had ended.

The *Sun Duchess* had departed Port Everglades three hours

late because a raccoon had turned up berserk in the pastry kitchen. One of the chefs had wrestled the frothing critter into a sixty-gallon tin of guava custard before it had shredded the man's jowls and humped snarling to the depths of the ship. A capture team from Broward Animal Control had arrived, along with health inspectors and paramedics. Evacuated passengers were appeased with rum drinks and canapés. Later, while reboarding, Joey had passed the Animal Control officers trudging empty-handed down the gangplank.

"I bet they couldn't catch it," she'd whispered to her husband. Despite the inconvenience caused by the raccoon, she'd found herself rooting for the addled little varmint.

"Rabies," her husband had said knowingly. "Damn thing lays a claw on me, I'll own this frigging cruise line."

"Oh, please, Chaz."

"From then on, you can call me Onassis. Think I'm kidding?"

The *Sun Duchess* was 855 feet long and weighed a shade more than seventy thousand tons. Joey had learned this from a brochure she'd found in their stateroom. The itinerary included Puerto Rico, Nassau and a private Bahamian island that the cruise lines had purchased (rumor had it) from the widow of a dismembered heroin trafficker. The last port of call before the ship returned to Fort Lauderdale was to be Key West.

Chaz had selected the cruise himself, claiming it was a present for their wedding anniversary. The first evening he'd spent on the fantail, slicing golf balls into the ocean. Initially Joey had been annoyed that the *Sun Duchess* would offer a driving range, much less a fake rock-climbing wall and squash courts. She and Chaz could have stayed in Boca and done all that.

No less preposterous was the ship's tanning parlor, which received heavy traffic whenever the skies turned overcast. The cruise company wanted every passenger to return home with either a bronze glow or a crimson burn, proof of their seven days in the tropics.

As it turned out, Joey wound up scaling the rock wall and

taking full advantage of the other amenities, even the two-lane bowling alley. The alternative was to eat and drink herself sick, gluttony being the principal recreation aboard cruise liners. The *Sun Duchess* was renowned for its twenty-four-hour surf-and-turf buffets, and that's how Joey's husband had spent the hours between ports.

Pig, she thought, submerging to shed a clot of seaweed that had wrapped around her neck like a sodden Yule garland.

Each day's sunrise had brought a glistening new harbor, yet the towns and straw markets were drearily similar, as if designed and operated by a franchise. Joey had earnestly tried to be charmed by the native wares, though many appeared to have been crafted in Singapore or South Korea. And what would one do with a helmet conch clumsily retouched with nail polish? Or a coconut husk bearing a hand-painted likeness of Prince Harry?

So grinding was the role of tourist that Joey had found herself looking forward to visiting the ship's "unspoiled private island", as it had been touted in the brochure. Yet that, too, proved dispiriting. The cruise line had mendaciously renamed the place Rapture Key while making only a minimal effort at restoration. Roosters, goats and feral hogs were the predominant fauna, having outlasted the smuggler who had been raising them for banquet fare. The island's sugar-dough flats were pocked with hulks of sunken drug planes, and the only shells to be found along the tree-shorn beach were of the .45-caliber variety.

"I'm gonna rent a Jet Ski," Chaz had cheerily decreed.

"I'll try to find some shade," Joey had said, "and finish my book."

The distance between them remained wide and unexplored. By the time the *Sun Duchess* had reached Key West, Joey and Chaz were spending only about one waking hour a day together, an interval usually devoted to either sex or an argument. It was pretty much the same schedule they kept at home.

So much for the romantic latitudes, Joey had thought, wishing she felt sadder than she did.

When her husband had scampered off to "check out the action" at Mallory Square, she briefly considered seducing one of the cabin attendants, a fine Peruvian brute named Tico. Ultimately Joey had lost the urge, dismissing the crestfallen young fellow with a peck on the chin and a fifty-dollar tip. She didn't feel strongly enough about Chaz to cheat on him even out of spite, although she suspected he'd cheated on her often (and quite possibly during the cruise).

Upon returning to the *Sun Duchess*, Chaz had been as chatty as a cockatoo on PCP.

"See all those clouds? It's about to rain," he'd proclaimed with a peculiar note of elation.

"I guess that means no golf tonight," Joey had said.

"Hey, I counted twenty-six T-shirt shops on Duval Street. No wonder Hemingway blew his brains out."

"That wasn't here," Joey had informed him. "That was in Idaho."

"How about some chow? I could eat a whale."

At dinner Chaz had kept refilling Joey's wineglass, over her protests. Now she understood why.

She felt it, too, that dehydrated alcohol fatigue. She'd been kicking hard up the crests of the waves and then breast-stroking down the troughs, but now she was losing both her rhythm and stamina. This wasn't the heated Olympic pool at UCLA; it was the goddamn Atlantic Ocean. Joey scrunched her eyelids to dull the saltwater burn.

I had a feeling he didn't love me anymore, she thought, but this is ridiculous.

Chaz Perrone listened for a splash but heard nothing except the deep lulling rumble of the ship's engines. Head cocked slightly, he stood at the rail as solitary and motionless as a heron.

He hadn't planned to toss her here. He had hoped to do it earlier in the voyage, somewhere between Nassau and San Juan, with the expectation that the currents would carry her body into Cuban waters, safely out of U.S. jurisdiction.

If the bull sharks didn't find her first.

Unfortunately, the weather had been splendid during that early leg of the cruise, and every night the outside decks were crowded with moony-eyed couples. Chaz's scheme required seclusion and he'd nearly abandoned hope, when the rain arrived, three hours after leaving Key West. It was only a drizzle, but Chaz knew it would drive the tourists indoors, stampeding for the lobster salad and electronic poker machines.

The second crucial element of his plot was surprise, Joey being a physically well-tuned woman and Chaz himself being somewhat softer and out of shape. Before luring her toward the stern of the *Sun Duchess* under the ruse of a starlit stroll, he'd made certain that his wife had consumed plenty of red wine; four and a half glasses, by his count. Two was usually enough to make her drowsy.

"Chaz, it's sprinkling," she had observed as they approached the rail.

Naturally she'd been puzzled, knowing how her husband despised getting wet. The man owned no fewer than seven umbrellas.

Pretending not to hear her, he had guided Joey forward by the elbow. "My stomach's a disaster. I think it's time they retired that seviche, don't you?"

"Let's go back inside," Joey had suggested.

From a pocket of his blue blazer Chaz had surreptitiously removed the key to their stateroom and let it fall to the polished planks at his feet. "Oops."

"Chaz, it's getting chilly out here."

"I think I dropped our key," he'd said, stooping to find it. Or so Joey had assumed.

He could only guess what had shot through his wife's mind when she'd felt him grab her ankles. *He's gotta be kidding,* is what she'd probably thought.

The act itself was a rudimentary exercise in leverage, really, flipping her backward over the rail. It had happened so fast, she hadn't made a peep.

As for the splash, Chaz would have preferred to hear it; a soft punctuation to the marriage and the crime. Then again, it was a long way down to the water.

He allowed himself a brief glance, but saw only whitecaps and foam in the rolling reflection of the ship's lights. The *Sun Duchess* kept moving, which was a relief. No Klaxons sounded.

Chaz picked up the key and hurried to the stateroom, bolting the door behind him. After hanging up his blazer, he opened another bottle of wine, poured some into two glasses and drank half of each.

Joey's suitcase lay open for re-packing, and Chaz moved it from the bed to the floor. He splayed his own travel bag and went foraging for an antacid. Beneath a stack of neatly folded boxers—Joey was a champion packer, he had to admit—Chaz came upon a box wrapped in tartan-style gift paper with green ribbon.

Inside the box was a gorgeous set of leather golf-club covers that were embossed with his initials, C.R.P. There was also a card: "Happy 2nd Anniversary! Love always, Joey."

Admiring the silken calfskin sheaths, Chaz felt a knot of remorse in his gut. It passed momentarily, like acid reflux.

His wife had class, no doubt about it. If only she hadn't been so damn . . . observant.

In exactly six hours he would report her missing.

Chaz stripped to his underwear and lobbed his clothes in a corner. Packed inside his carry-on was a paperback edition of *Madame Bovary*, which he opened randomly and placed for effect on the nightstand by Joey's side of the bed.

Then Charles Regis Perrone set his alarm clock, laid his head on the pillow and went to sleep.

The Gulf Stream carried Joey northward at almost four knots. She knew she'd have to swim harder if she didn't want to end up bloated and rotting on some sandbar in North Carolina.

But, Lord, she was tired.

Had to be the wine. Chaz knew she wasn't much of a drinker, and obviously he'd planned it all in advance. Probably hoped that the fall from the ship would break her legs or knock her unconscious, and if it didn't, so what? She'd be miles from land in a pitching black ocean, and scared shitless. Nobody would find her even if they went looking, and she'd drown from exhaustion before daylight.

That's what Chaz probably figured.

He hadn't forgotten about her glory days at UCLA, either, Joey realized. He knew she would start swimming, if she somehow survived the fall. In fact, he was counting on her to swim; betting that his stubborn and prideful wife would wear herself out when she should have tucked into a floating position and conserved her strength until sunrise. At least then she'd have a speck of a chance to be seen by a passing ship.

Sometimes I wonder about myself, Joey thought.

Once a tanker passed so close that it blocked out the moon. The ship's silhouette was squat and dark and squared at both ends, like a high-rise condo tipped on its side. Joey had hollered and waved, but there was no chance of being heard above the clatter of the engines. The tanker pushed by, a russet wall of noise and fumes, and Joey resumed swimming.

Soon her legs started going numb, a spidery tingle that began in her toes and crept upward. Muscle cramps wouldn't have surprised her, but the slow deadening did. She found herself laboring to keep her face above the waves, and eventually she sensed that she'd stopped kicking altogether. Toward the end she switched to the breaststroke, her legs trailing like pale broken cables.

We've only been married two years, she was thinking. What did I do to deserve *this*?

To take her mind off dying, Joey composed a mental list of the things that Chaz didn't like about her:

1. She tended to overcook fowl, particularly chicken, due to a lifelong fear of salmonella.

2. The facial moisturizing cream that she applied at night smelled vaguely like insecticide.

3. Sometimes she dozed off during hockey games, even the play-offs.

4. She refused to go down on him while he was driving on Interstate 95, the Sunshine State Parkway or any surface road where the posted speed limit exceeded fifty miles per hour.

5. She could whip him at tennis whenever she felt like it.

6. She occasionally "misplaced" his favorite George Thorogood CDs.

7. She declined to entertain the possibility of inviting his hairstylist over for a threesome.

8. She belonged to a weekly book group.

9. She had more money than he did.

10. She brushed with baking soda instead of toothpaste . . .

Come on, Joey thought.

A guy doesn't suddenly decide to murder his wife just because she serves a chewy Cornish hen.

Maybe it's another woman, Joey thought. But then why not just ask me for a divorce?

She didn't have the energy to sort it all out. She'd married a worthless horndog and now he'd heaved her overboard on their anniversary cruise and very soon she would drown and be devoured by sharks. Out here you had the big boys: blacktips, lemons, hammerheads, tigers, makos and bulls . . .

Please, God, don't let them eat me, Joey thought, until after I've died.

The same warm tingle was starting in her fingertips and soon, she knew, both arms would be as spent and useless as her legs. Her lips had gone raw from the salt, her tongue was swollen like a kielbasa and her eyelids were puffy and crusted. Still, the lights of Florida beckoned like stardust whenever she reached the top of a wave.

So Joey struggled on, believing she still had a slender chance of survival. If she made it across the Gulf Stream, she'd finally be able to rest; ball up and float until the sun came up.

She had momentarily forgotten about the sharks, when something heavy and rough-skinned butted against her left breast. Thrashing and grunting, she beat at the thing with both fists until the last of her strength was gone.

Cavitating into unconsciousness, she was subjected to a flash vision of Chaz in their stateroom aboard the *Sun Duchess*, screwing a blonde croupier before heading aft for one final bucket of balls.

132

Prick, Joey thought.

Then the screen in her head went blank.

*

At heart Chaz Perrone was irrefutably a cheat and a maggot, but he had always shunned violence as dutifully as a Quaker elder. Nobody who knew him, including his few friends, would have imagined him capable of homicide. Chaz himself was somewhat amazed that he'd gone through with it.

When the alarm clock went off, he awoke with the notion that he'd imagined the whole scene. Then he rolled over and saw that Joey's side of the bed was empty. Through the porthole he spied the jetties that marked the entrance of Port Everglades, and he knew he wasn't dreaming. He had definitely killed his wife.

Chaz was dazzled by his own composure. He reached for the phone, made the call he'd been practicing and prepared himself for what was to come. He gargled lightly but otherwise made no attempt at personal grooming, dishevelment being expected of a frantic husband.

Soon after the *Sun Duchess* docked, the interviews commenced. First to arrive was the ship's solicitous security chief, then a pair of baby-faced Coast Guard officers and finally a dyspeptic Broward County Sheriff's detective. Meanwhile, the *Sun Duchess* was being combed from bow to stern, presumably to rule out the embarrassing possibility that Mrs. Perrone was shacking up with another passenger or, worse, a crew member.

"Exactly what time did your wife leave the stateroom?" the detective asked.

"Three-thirty in the morning," Chaz said.

The specificity of the lie was important to ensure that the rescue operation would focus on the wrong swatch of ocean. The ship's location at 3:30 a.m. would have been approximately seventy miles north of the spot where he'd tumbled his wife overboard.

"And you say she was going to 'scope out' the moon?" the detective asked.

"That's what she told me." Chaz had been rubbing his eyes to keep them red and bleary, as befitting a hungover, anxiety-stricken spouse. "I must've nodded off. When I woke up, the sun was rising and the ship was pulling into port and Joey still wasn't back. That's when I phoned for help."

The detective, a pale and icy Scandinavian type, jotted a single sentence in his notebook. He pointed at the two wineglasses next to the bed. "She didn't finish hers."

"No." Chaz sighed heavily.

"Or take it with her. Wonder why."

"We'd already had a whole bottle at dinner."

"Yes, but still," the detective said, "you're going out to look at the moon, most women would bring their wine. Some might even bring their husbands."

Chaz cautiously measured his response. He hadn't expected to get his balls busted so early in the game.

"Joey asked me to meet her on the Commodore Deck and I told her I'd bring our wineglasses," Chaz said. "But I fell asleep instead— okay, make that passed out. We'd had quite a lot to drink, actually."

"More than one bottle, then."

"Oh yeah."

"Would you say your wife was intoxicated?"

Chaz shrugged gloomily.

"Did you two have an argument last night?" the detective asked.

"Absolutely not." It was the only true piece of Chaz's story.

"Then why didn't you go outside together?"

"Because I was sittin' on the can, okay? Taking care of some personal business." Chaz tried to make himself blush. "The seviche they fed us last night, let me just say, tasted like something the cat yakked up. So I told Joey, 'Go ahead without me, I'll be along in a few minutes.' "

"Bringing the wineglasses with you."

"That's right. But instead I must've laid down and passed out," Chaz said. "So, yeah, it's basically all my fault."

"What's your fault?" the detective asked mildly.

Chaz experienced a momentary tightness in his chest. "If

anything bad happened to Joey, I mean. Who else is there to blame but myself?"

"Why?"

"Because I shouldn't have let her go out so late by herself. You think I don't know that? You think I don't feel a hundred percent responsible?"

The detective closed his notebook and got up. "Maybe nothing happened to your wife, Mr. Perrone. Maybe she'll turn up safe and sound."

"God, I hope so."

The detective smiled emptily. "It's a big ship."

And even a bigger ocean, thought Chaz.

"One more question. Has Mrs. Perrone been acting depressed lately?"

Chaz gave a brittle laugh and raised both his palms. "Don't even start with that! Joey definitely was *not* suicidal. No way. Ask anybody who knew her—"

"*Knows* her," the detective interjected.

"Right. She's the most positive person you'll ever meet." The emphatic response was meant to strengthen Chaz's position with the authorities. He knew from his amateur research that relatives of suicide victims commonly deny seeing prior symptoms of depression.

The detective said, "Sometimes, when people drink—"

"Yeah, but not Joey," Chaz broke in. "Drinking gave her—gives her—the giggles."

Chaz realized he'd been gnawing on his lower lip, which actually turned out to be a fine touch. It made him appear truly worried about his missing wife.

The detective picked up the copy of *Madame Bovary*. "Yours or hers?"

"Hers." Chaz was pleased that the bait had been taken.

"No giggles here," the detective remarked, glancing at the open pages.

"I haven't read it," Chaz said, which was true. He had asked the clerk at the Barnes & Noble for something romantic but tragic.

"It's about a lady who gets misunderstood by just about

everybody, including herself," the detective said. "Then she swallows arsenic."

Perfect, Chaz thought. "Look, Joey was happy last night," he said, not quite as insistently. "Why else would she dash out at three-thirty in the morning to go dancing on the deck?"

"In the moonlight."

"Correct."

"The captain said he ran into some rain."

"Yes, but that was earlier," Chaz said. "About eleven or so. By the time Joey went out, it was beautiful."

Before the *Sun Duchess* had departed Key West, Chaz had checked the weather radar on TV at a famous bar called Sloppy Joe's. He had known that the skies would be clear by 3:30 a.m., the fabricated time of his wife's disappearance.

"The moon was full last night," Chaz added, to give the false impression that he'd seen it himself.

"I believe that's right," the detective said.

He stood there as if he were expecting Chaz to say more.

So Chaz did. "I just remembered something else. There was a raccoon, a rabid raccoon, running loose on the ship."

"Yes."

"I'm serious. Ask the captain. We were held up for hours leaving Lauderdale last Sunday while they looked for it."

"Go on."

"Well, don't you see? What if Joey got attacked when she went out on the deck? What if that deranged little monster went chasing after her and she accidentally fell overboard or something?"

The detective said, "That's quite a theory."

"You ever seen an animal with rabies? They get totally whacked."

"I already know about the raccoon," said the detective. "They trapped it in the crew's laundry and removed it from the ship at San Juan, according to the captain's log."

"Oh," Chaz said. "Well, it's good you checked that out."

"We try to be thorough." This was spoken in a barbed tone that Chaz felt was inappropriate for use on a distraught husband. He was glad when the detective finally departed, and further relieved to learn that he was free to start packing. The stateroom had to be vacated soon, as the *Sun Duchess* was being prepared for its next cruise.

Later, as Chaz Perrone followed the porter down the gangway, he saw two blaze-orange helicopters rising from a pad at the Coast Guard station on the other side of the port. The choppers banked and sped off toward the Atlantic, where a cutter and two smaller rescue vessels were already hunting in grids for Joey. The Coasties would also be sending up a Falcon out of Opa-locka, or so Chaz had been assured.

He glanced at his watch and thought: Thirteen hours in the drink, she's history.

They can search all they want.

Hank and Lana Wheeler lived in Elko, Nevada, where they owned a prosperous casino resort that featured a Russian dancing-bear act. The bears were raised and trained by a semi-retired dominatrix who billed herself as Ursa Major.

Over time the Wheelers had become fond of Ursa and treated her as kin. When one of her star performers, a 425-pound neutered Asiatic named Boris, developed an impacted bicuspid, the Wheelers generously chartered a Gulfstream jet to transport the animal to a renowned periodontic veterinarian at Lake Tahoe. Hank and Lana went along for moral support, and also to sneak in some spring skiing.

On the return flight something went sour and the plane nosedived into the Cortez Mountains. Federal investigators later determined that, for reasons unknown, the convalescing bear had been seated in the co-pilot's position at the time of the crash. Film recovered from a 35-mm camera owned by the Wheelers revealed several snapshots of Boris squeezed upright behind the steering yoke. In one frame, Ursa Major was curled laughingly on the beast's lap, tipping a bottle of Bailey's Irish Cream to its unfurled lips. In a subsequent photo, Boris had been posed in headphones and tinted aviator glasses.

Taped communications between the Gulfstream and control towers en route confirmed a highly festive, and possibly distracting, atmosphere aboard the Wheelers' jet. Why it had suddenly gone down remained a mystery, though Ursa's assistant surmised that the bear's sunny humor had evaporated dramatically once the Xylocaine wore off. During the aircraft's fatal corkscrew plummet, controllers attempting to radio the cockpit received only bestial snorts and grunts in reply.

The Wheelers were worth a pile of money, which after probate was divided evenly between their two young children. Joey Wheeler, who had been named after the singer-actress Joey Heatherton, was only four years old when her parents died. Her brother, named after the comedian Corbett Monica, was six. Each of the kids came immediately into approximately $4 million, plus a guaranteed cut of the weekly keno handle at their late parents' casino.

Joey and Corbett were raised in Southern California by Lana Wheeler's twin sister, who conspired zealously but without success to loot the trust fund in which the children's inheritance had been placed. Consequently, both orphaned Wheelers reached adulthood with their fortunes intact but their innocence abraded.

Corbett lit out for New Zealand, while Joey headed to Florida. There she informed no one of her wealth, including the stockbroker who would become her first husband. She and Benjamin Middenbock dated for five years and were married for four more, until fate intervened in the form of a sky diver who fell on Benny one sunny afternoon as he practiced fly casting in the backyard. The sky diver's parachute had failed to open and he had descended silently, though like a sack of cement, upon Joey's husband, who had been breaking in a new Loomis 9-weight. The tragedy left Joey alone, stupefied and richer than ever, thanks to a seven-figure settlement check from the skydiving company's insurance carrier.

It was the second time in her young life that she had unwillingly profited from the death of loved ones, and she could scarcely bring herself to think about the money, much less put a dent in it. Misplaced guilt led her into charity work and a modest lifestyle, though she had retained a weakness for

Italian shoes. Joey Wheeler hoped someday to establish a regular life among regular people, or at least to find out if such an existence was possible.

She met Chaz Perrone one January afternoon in a parking lot outside the Animal Kingdom attraction at Walt Disney World, where she'd just made a flying tackle on a teenager who had swiped the purse of a Belgian tourist. The culprit, who belonged to a group of youths being chaperoned by Joey, supposedly had been diagnosed with chronic attention deficit disorder. Oddly, the young man's capacity for concentration was not so diminished that he'd failed to focus on a genuine Prada handbag amid the heaving throngs of tourists. Nor had his focus wavered even slightly as he stalked his elderly victim from the Giant Anteater exhibit all the way to DinoLand, where he'd made the snatch.

Joey had chased the pimpled creep through the ticket turnstiles and brought him down hard on the hot pavement outside the park.

While holding him for Disney security officers, she'd shaken from his pockets a Gucci key chain and a Tiffany cigarette lighter, casting further doubt on the nature of his disability.

Chaz Perrone, having watched the takedown from a departing tram, had hopped off to compliment Joey on her pluck. She'd found him impossibly handsome, and had done nothing to discourage the flirtation. Chaz had proudly informed her that he was a biologist, and that he was attending a convention of distinguished scientists working to save the Everglades. He'd further confided that he was supposed to be taking a VIP safari tour of the Animal Kingdom but was instead sneaking out to play Bay Hill, the favorite hometown golf course of none other than Tiger Woods.

Joey had been attracted to Chaz not only by his good looks, but by his involvement in such a lofty mission as rescuing Florida's imperiled wilderness from greedy polluters. At the time he'd seemed like a fine catch, though in retrospect Joey realized that her judgment had been skewed by previous disappointments. Before meeting Chaz, she had been dumped in chilly succession by a tennis pro, a lifeguard and a defrocked pharmacist, a grim streak that destabilized her self-esteem as well as her standards.

So she'd been eager, if not reckless, for steady companionship. The courtship had been a whirlwind campaign of roses, love letters, candle-lit dinners, whispered endearments; Chaz had been relentlessly smooth, and Joey had melted with minimal resistance. Her most distinct memories of their first twelve months of marriage were scenes of reliably torrid sex, which turned out to be Chaz's singular shining talent. It was also his obsession. During their more revelatory second year together, Joey came to realize that she'd mistaken her husband's indefatigable urge to rut for ardor, when, in truth, for him it was no more personal than isometrics. She also became acutely aware that Chaz did not regard matrimony as an exclusive carnal arrangement.

Other wives might have bailed out, but Joey was too proud and competitive. She resolved to immerse herself avidly in all aspects of her husband's world, and to become what the self-help books called "a true life partner." Her plan was to make Chaz need her so fervidly that he'd knock off the bullshit and clean up his act.

The anniversary cruise seemed like a good opportunity to put her plan into action, so Joey had accepted the invitation with high hopes. She had looked forward to "re-connecting" with her husband, as the relationship experts advised. The biggest challenge would be engaging Chaz in at least one intimate conversation that did not concern the peerless durability of his erection.

Once at sea, unfortunately, the breakthrough moment had never presented itself. Or perhaps it had and Joey had found herself not sufficiently motivated. Except for the sex, Chaz simply wasn't a very compelling fellow. The more Joey had listened to him—*really* listened—the emptier she'd felt. For a scientist, Chaz seemed dishearteningly blithe, self-centered and materialistic. He rarely spoke of his work in the Everglades, and he seemed largely unfazed by the rape of the planet. He displayed no anger about the push for oil drilling in an Alaskan wildlife refuge, yet he bitched for a solid hour, spewing half-masticated shreds of clam, upon hearing from another cruise passenger that Titleist was raising the price of its golf balls.

It had struck Joey that she could spend the rest of her life faking enthusiasm for her husband's interests, and that he wouldn't care one way or the other. So, why in the world had he married her? Joey had intended to pose that very question during their late-night stroll on the *Sun Duchess*, but then she'd changed her mind. The slate clouds and the drizzling rain had depressed her, and all she'd wanted to do was go back to the room and crash.

She'd been staring off toward Africa, thinking of God knows what, when Chaz bent down to pick up something he'd dropped on the deck; a key, he'd said. Joey had been perturbed to feel his moist hands closing around her ankles— she'd figured he was about to spread her legs so he could slip her a fast one, Chaz being keen on outdoor quickies. The last thing she had expected him to do was throw her overboard.

The worthless shithead, Joey thought.

Because here I am, parched and delirious and half-blind, clinging to the same fucking shark that tried to eat me.

Which is absolutely ludicrous, so I must either be dead or getting damn close. . . .

He knew he couldn't get his hands on the money, even if something happened to me. He knew from day one that my inheritance was untouchable. So why did he do this?

It made no sense to Joey Perrone. Nothing did.

Not Chaz; not the lazy, sweet-smelling, rough-skinned shark; not the seagulls piping excitedly overhead—can't a person even die in peace?

Not the low *chug-a-chug* of an outboard engine, growing louder; not the slappety-slap of the waves against . . . what, the hull of a boat? Don't believe your ears, Joey told herself. What would a boat be doing all the way out here?

Didn't make sense. Neither did the faraway voice calling to her, a man's voice urging her to hang on, honey, just hang on for another minute.

Then the same voice saying it's okay, I've got you now, so let go, come on, let it go!

Something lifted her as if she were as light and free as a bubble. Glassy droplets streamed down her bare legs as she rose from the water, her toes brushing the foamy tips of the waves.

Then came a huddled warmth, the smell of dry linen and a sleep nearly as deep as death.

PARADISE

BY A. L. KENNEDY

Happiness is not a state that A. L. Kennedy writes about habitually, so the fact that her latest work is called *Paradise* is intriguing. This book is positively wringing with melancholy, despair, self-delusion and hopelessness, but is poignant, heartrending and as addictive as the liquor that fuels the story. Hannah Luckraft has spent her life hiding from herself; from her own personal demons; from the questions posed by the world around her; from life itself. Her shield has been drink: to her, this is no problem. Life is better when she drinks, drink is not the problem, life is the problem and drink makes it easier to live. When she tries to stop, it is not for herself, but those who despairingly love her, those she has let down because they had unrealistic expectations that she could be just like them. Hannah finds a kindred spirit in Robert, a disillusioned dentist with an ex-wife and child but the hope offered by this love is dependent upon the drink that fuels them together and apart. Offering no solutions or prospect of happy endings, *Paradise* is written as an uncertain, inter-rupted stream of consciousness.

Born and educated in Scotland, A. L. Kennedy is perhaps better known for her short story collections of which the sublime *Original Bliss* is a great example, but it can only be a matter of time before she comes of age as a novelist and joins the top rank of British literary writers. This could well be the book that catapults her to that plane. Using her short story skills to compose a patchwork of incidents that make up the whole, hauntingly beautiful and nakedly sad, *Paradise* is a novel about the vulnerability of being human and the fear of living that exists in all of us.

Recommended by Mike Cooper,
Waterstone's Tunbridge Wells

£14.99
ISBN: 0224062581
Published September 2004

But as long as I'm making progress, that's the thing. And, like everyone else, I do – racking up the days, night after morning, I am achieving time. Which is a modest accomplishment, I know, but I don't take it for granted.

Because I was born with the absolute certainty that I would die before leaving thirty. I arrived with ten toes and blue eyes and death firmly in mind. I passed the age when lives should be taken in hand, knowing that no such formalities would be required. For me, there would be no pension, no insurance, no prudent mortgage plan, no fretting over outrages in homes for the elderly, or the ultimate loss of my health and faculties. I was carefree.

And completely wrong, of course.

As of now, I should be six years, eight months and a few days dead. In reality, it looks not unlikely that I'll make forty in due course.

But this is largely good news: for instance, by trusting in what has become a false goal I've still generated an undoubted onward drive and saved myself much useless introspection and unease. I have reached my current position in spite – or even because – of my steadfast denials that I ever could. And my very reasonable unwillingness to bother planning activities beyond my predicted demise has allowed my current lifestyle to excel in improvisation and has encouraged many happy accidents.

I first meet Robert, after all, when I am already years overdue for the grave. Seeing him again, beginning to learn his

145

hands, spending the whole of the following day with the taste of him under my teeth – this also happens totally by chance.

For three weeks after that, of course, he doesn't phone and nor do I, not having his number – or, indeed, the necessary lack of pride to make the call.

And, right now, I'm thinking of Robert and his failings – or possibly mine. I am wondering why it was so easy to be comfortable and friendly when he finally did call, why the two of us decided three weeks could be nothing at all. Meanwhile, I am rolling quickly, irresistibly, close to forty and speeding across the flanks of my present day. I am also standing very still in the doorway of a barn, dizzied with remembered time, the smothering in of my past.

Beyond the lintel's shade, there is the sweetness of grain fields on the breeze, the bland dust of poor soil, baked to a yellowish crust: and salt, too: something of the high-tide line, bladderwrack and rock clefts dank with scrub and gorse: that slightly human, musty fug of heated gorse, the snap of its seeds, the blood drop in the yellow of each flower: which is to say, the smell and taste and everything of my being a child in summer, of running between the blue, narrow shore and the racing depths of barley with my brother until the sun had fallen and the sandy earth was cooled to match the temperature of skin.

I used to be young here. This is where days and days of me were played out harmlessly.

But back to business.

There always will be something to interrupt.

I clear my throat and blink and become what is now expected – an adult selling cardboard to another adult – what a life. 'How many, then?'

'Eh?'

I hate farmers. 'How many do you want?' Especially this farmer.

'Eh?'

No, what I hate are soft-fruit farmers who order a piss-poor handful of 6lb pick-your-own baskets and then lapse into fainting fits and vapours when trails of hapless civilians use, wreck, steal and otherwise outstrip available supplies.

*The baskets are for people to put fruit in – so fruit is going to be put in them by people – that's what all your badly spelled, half-arsed, '****Come and Meet the Strawberries and Then Eat Their Children****' roadside placards are enticing them to do – what did you expect? That they'd bring their own sodding baskets? That they'd hand-plait wicker trugs the night before to save you expense? That they'd fill up their hats and trouser pockets and then go?*

'How many more, Mr Campbell?' We're near the start of the raspberry canes – which are already heaving with mums and dads and kiddies, plucking down enough fruit to keep Dante's inferno endlessly boiling with lakes of crimson jam. 'I mean, you've got what . . . two more weeks like this . . .? the currants . . . blackberries . . . you know how long they'll last . . .'

Farmer Campbell stares at me as if the blackberries are my fault, a distress I have engineered. Then his gaze clatters down to my ankles and twitches about. He frowns and begins to shuffle across the yard towards his house. 'I'll go in and think, like. I'll go in and think.'

He's doing this because I was late, unavoidably delayed on a mission of mercy, but Farmer Campbell doesn't know that: he simply wants to make a point. I delay him and then he delays me. Here I am, offering him uniquely environmental, recyclable, sturdy cardboard baskets – no nasty metal handles, our patented safe and biodegradable webbing instead – and he can't even offer a coffee, never mind a glass of something pleasant, or a firm order. I bet his strawberries are shite, anyway. Every grower I know is producing these weird, new varieties: the fruit keeps well, packs well, freezes well, travels well, shows well – but then you try to eat it and it tastes like wet bicycle tyres, I mean what is the point ?

There's a boy shuffling up between the rows of canes – his basket is too heavy for him and he's lunging it forward, then resting it on the ground and picking again, serious, fingers bloody with juice and maybe slightly scratched. When my mother took us to the fields, Simon would be like that: never ate any himself, only solemnly gathered monster amounts of raspberries, because they were his favourite. Mine, too. We used to have a lot in common, even though he could be so stern to his appetites.

Down at the weighing-out scales, I'd be gorged with fruit, almost nauseous, Mother smiling slyly about it – my greed and waste of growing things providing their own punishment. Simon would be grim behind me, struggling with his mounded load, but wanting nobody to help, because this was his business, something he had done. The weigher would wink, or look at him with a nice touch of awe as the scale's needle bounced straight over to some miraculous total for a lad of such tender years and I would try to hate my brother for being someone who was better than me and then I would see the thin lines of blood on his forearms and his fingers, the beaded tracks where the thorns had caught him, and I would be defeated, I would be proud. My little brother being sore and hot and tired, but finishing what he'd started, anyway – if you couldn't be proud of yourself, then you could be proud of Simon.

Still no sign of Campbell.

Five more minutes and I will leave, drive off: the Cardboard Products Group does not need this kind of dilettante custom. CPG's lovely, moulded punnets, self-ventilating single-layer fruit trays and other wholesomely practical containers will no longer be made available to Castlerigg Farm. In fact, Castlerigg Farm can screw itself, along with its owner – he's already using someone else's punnets in any case – nasty plastic ones, I spotted a pile of them in a shed. Farmer Campbell clearly has no concern for the well-being of our planet.

Strictly speaking, CPG may not either. I remain unconvinced by our figures for recycled pulp incorporation and some of our boxes come from Indonesia, for Christ's sake: China. I feel they may not be ethically produced – more like pure, compressed rainforest cut into sheets and then probably put together by limbless tykes in cellars full of rats.

Not that it's any concern of mine, I only sell the stuff.

Although I am basically altruistic and do my bit in other ways – hence my tardy arrival at Castlerigg this afternoon. I was sidetracked by being humanitarian, which takes time.

I'd pulled up in one of those little Fife towns: sternly picturesque buildings full of cousins intent on impoverishing their gene pools. I'd found the usual post office-cum-news-agent-cum-bakery (the standard range of products plus peat briquettes, half a dozen dodgy videos for sale on a back shelf, some small and probably stolen electrical goods) and I had bought two flattened ham and salad baps for breakfast, a newspaper and a styrofoam cup of coffee that smelled uncannily like sweat.

There was a small, abused park nearby and I went and sat in it for my meal, admiring the rustic sandstone bridge (spray-painted with charmless expletives, mainly in blue) and the tinkling brook (rich both in weedy nooks and bottles that once contained a cheap, fortified wine). I ignored each unpleasant detail and attempted to be at peace.

Except that over the road an elderly woman was labouring to escape what I could guess was her own garden gate. She had obviously suffered a stroke at some time and had little or no strength on her right side. Her left hand was leaning heavily on a wheelchair, while she tried to push the gate open with her back. The hinges were proving intransigent. There was a deep weariness in the woman's face that seemed to suggest she fought like this every day, took so long about so many things every day that she could no longer afford to acknowledge how intolerable this was.

Which is the sort of thing that shouldn't happen: the sort of thing that comes from lack of thought. Some moron in an office somewhere doles out a bloody wheelchair to a fellow human being who hasn't the use of both arms – and how is that human being supposed to get into the chair, out of it, and how are they supposed to push themselves about? Office Moron can't imagine, doesn't want to; as far as Office Moron is concerned a person who can't walk has been issued with a wheelchair, problem solved.

This sort of stupidity makes me angry, how could it not?

Needless to say, I abandoned my snack and nipped across to offer help, hold open the gate while the old dear tottered herself down and into the chair. I smiled what I could feel was a very good smile and, as if she had felt it, she glanced up and gave me a painstaking nod.

By this stage, I could tell that she meant to scoot herself along the pavement backwards, using her good foot – this being, no doubt, her best bet for getting around – what else could she manage unaided? Still, it seemed to be incredibly dangerous and undignified and I wasn't in any hurry to turn up *chez Campbell* and discuss baskets so why not behave as anyone decent would and offer, 'I could push you, if you'd like? I'm just having a break – nothing much to do. Would that be okay?'

I could see that she understood me, but no longer had words to hand. Her body relaxed, though, as soon as she heard my suggestion, slipped back, and I got this half-grin from her – a half being all she could muster.

'Is it this way? The shops? You just point, can you?'

I wasn't going to get a chat, clearly, and I didn't want to blather away as I might to a baby, or a dog – the usual things you meet that can't answer back. Still, there was no call for me to be stand-offish. Having care of a whole other human body like that, noticing every incline and the tiny irregularities in the pavement as they jar up through the handles of the chair – with so much going on in that weird, mechanical-intimate sort of way, you can't just ignore your companion and plod along behind them without trying to break the ice.

'You know I don't have a licence for one of these . . .'

I couldn't tell if that amused her or not. She made what seemed a happy noise inside her throat.

I wouldn't have thought it, but she was actually quite a weight, took a bit of shoving from time to time and I was starting to be rather heated, which wasn't good news for the hair and the business suit – and I favour this suit: chalk-stripe on a grey wool mix, mildly tailored jacket and skirt, matched with a boring, white blouse and librarian's shoes. My reliable ensemble. No need to be troubled about it, though: not when

I also had that pleasant, proprietorial warmth growing out around me.

I am a stranger helping a stranger – this can still happen. It's nice. I'm nice.

On the other hand, people were passing us by, here and there, and these were possibly people who knew her. She must be a bit of a character, a landmark, after all: kicking along arse-forwards, day after day: a bit of hazard to watch for, in fact. Most of the town must have recognised her, but me – I was an unknown quantity, perhaps an object of distrust. I was a visiting Samaritan, caring in a way that they would not, but I felt them study me, nonetheless: a tangible, quizzical frisk of interest as each one walked by, no sympathy in it, no fellow feeling.

And I could appreciate their point of view. In a sense, I was abducting this old lady, I was pushing her off without proper introductions. I had no special training, or experience. Good will, I was full of – but who still has any faith in that?

I gentled her down the slope at a kerb and waited, over-cautiously, for every scrap of traffic to move far out of sight. 'Still okay, then? Straight on when we get over?' Her good arm wags to the right. 'Down there? Okey-dokey. Down there it is.'

I never say *okey-dokey*. I don't think anyone else does, either.

We trundled on and the pressure of the town which was, no doubt, staring after, made the hairs lift on my neck. I was beginning to feel undermined. Members of caring professions, they were au fait with wheelchairs and stretchers, trolleys, propelling the vulnerable with efficiency and calm. I didn't know about this, I was guessing, my role was not a comfortable fit.

Onwards, though, onwards. 'Are you visiting a pal, then? Going to a centre? A shop?' The street was narrow: non-descript terraces hemming us in from either side: dirty-white harling and bad windows, closed doors. 'Just out for a wander, are you?' Which was possible, she had the right to go out and ramble, like any pedestrian. Of course, this meant that I could be condemned to pushing her round for the rest of the day.

Or we could have been heading off in a quite incorrect direction. She might have been disorientated, lost. Somebody local might have noticed that I was taking this woman the wrong way. This might have caused them alarm.

I looked behind, but no one was following, there were no visible observers. Still, a definite scrutiny tickled my shoulders, perhaps from someone discreetly in pursuit. I tried to hope I was mistaken and pressed on.

A weak, little sound rose up to me then and I realised the woman in the chair was humming, singing away to herself and looking about and pleased with making no kind of effort as we progressed. So, whoever she was, she had warmed to me, to my smile, and I was letting her have a good start to her day. It didn't matter who was on our trail – we had nothing to hide.

A few paces on and she motioned we should cross the road. The pavement was of the old-fashioned type, elevated, the kerb only descending to the gutter by way of three shallow steps. This meant I would have to multiply the manoeuvre I'd used across previous kerbstones by three, which would be simple but strenuous.

I turned her softly, pitched the chair towards me by a minor angle and then rolled the back wheels over and down the first step without trouble.

I looked at the next steps.

I stopped.

I had to.

Because then I clearly understood what a lovely, put-upon, old lady she was and what a jolly time she was having.

And because then I also clearly understood how terrible it was going to be when I didn't do this properly and dropped her.

I was going to drop her.

I could tell.

I hadn't a clue what I was doing. I had no advice. There was no way things were going to turn out well here.

The lady, she was terribly helpless and fragile and wonderful and no human person like that could be left to rely on somebody like me. I was going to ruin this and harm her when I did. This would be my fault. I wouldn't mean it, but that wouldn't change how sad it was going to be.

My grip was cooling, sliding, on the handles of the chair and the accident was coming, but I couldn't wait for it. I couldn't bear that it wasn't here yet. I was getting upset.

So I did what I had to and opened my hands and the chair kicked forward, bounced, jolted down the second step, while the woman's good hand darted up, trying to ward off the coming sadness, and then there was the quicker roll and thudded landing from the lowest step, her unbalanced trajectory that curved fast across the road, the chair still upright – amazingly upright, and thank God for the lack of traffic – and then she reached the place where the one front wheel collided with the high kerb opposite and tipped the street into the noise of metal and overturning and her noise and the fall of her body and the way that her pale blue coat would be dirty now.

I ran over to her: I'm not a monster. I ran over and hugged her up and I'm sure she'd only sprained her wrist, and there was otherwise nothing much wrong, apart from this cut on her head, bleeding the way that a head wound does and me with nothing to stop it, not a handkerchief.

She looked at me and wasn't angry, although I'd thought she would be. Instead, she had this bewildered hurt in her eyes and the start of tears and a horrible, horrible loneliness.

'I'm sorry. I'm so sorry. I'm so sorry. I'll go and get someone. No, I have to. I'm sorry. You need someone to help me.' She held my hand. 'I'm sorry. I need help.'

But I didn't go. I stayed. I'm not a monster.

A minute, or five, or twenty later and a crowd had surrounded me, edged me back, and some housewife, still in slippers, had come out with a blanket, the blood colouring it at once – not too much, not a harmful loss, but definite staining, obvious blood.

I'd thought I would have to explain myself, but actually

nobody bothered much with me and, as I knew, the woman I had injured couldn't speak and was confused by the flow of events. She was unable to accuse, or even identify, me. So I allowed myself to be the passer-by who'd found her and then no one in particular, standing for a while and then a stranger who walked away as an ambulance siren echoed in.

I didn't want any of that to happen and I do hope she's all right, I truly hope she is all right. There's no way that I can explain how awful I feel, how guilty. But it was mostly a type of accident and act of God. I'm not a monster. If I'd really meant to harm her, I would be, but I didn't. Sometimes things are unavoidable.

I had to sit and ease in a brandy before I could drive here, to Castlerigg. I used a pub in another town, not that lady's – I won't go back there, couldn't take a drink in it again.

'Is there something the matter, hen?'

Farmer Campbell has soundlessly crossed his courtyard and is holding out a grubby mug of tea. He still seems to be fascinated by my feet and, when I glance down, I can see that my sensible, grey shoes are caked with blood and my tights are spattered. Under my jacket, my blouse is marked with it, I saw that, but I thought I'd washed the rest of it off in the pub toilet.

The stains are thick, glossy, like varnish.

I am not a monster, I only look like one.

'There was.' I take his tea. 'There was this accident I saw. I mean, I was there . . . I touched someone bleeding.'

'I kent there was something.'

'She'll be fine, though. She'll be fine, I'm sure. Sorry.'

Over by the farmhouse door, Mrs Campbell loiters, curious.

'Sorry.'

'No need to be sorry, hen.'

'Sorry.'

I don't know what will happen next.

But, as it turns out, Campbell will offer me the chance of a seat inside and will suggest that I shouldn't be driving. I will shake my head and stand where I am, aware of the burden of my shoes, their new heaviness, and I will swallow down his over-sweetened tea and then we will take his emergency order from my car and put it, clean and cellophane-wrapped, inside the straw-scented darkness of a barn. Campbell will ask me to fill out a form requesting another dozen packs of baskets, which I know is rather more than he really needs or wants to buy.

I am not a monster, but I will profit from my crime.

I will get into my car and follow its steering wheel as it leads me back through the shadowed, turning lanes and under the reddening sun and I will cross the long bridge home as the sky starts burning. My hand will be steady when I reach out to the booth and pay my toll and then I will pull away and take the bends and climbs that bring me to my street, my flat, my bathroom and the shower that I will run until the tank is empty, washing until I am cold, but not quite clean.

'What are you thinking?' Robert is a little smashed, but not as smashed as me.

'*What are you thinking?* – You always fucking say that, what does it *mean*? You're just pretending you already know something. Well, you don't.'

I am glad that we are together these days, together often, but there are times when he's here too much: too large, too loud, too dense. This is one of the times.

A fortnight ago, this bar was unfamiliar to us both, so we have started from scratch in here together, cultivated the ways it can welcome us, and now it is almost our place. So Robert is filling our place, my place, looming into it, blaring, drowning out the pleasant and peaceable atmosphere that comes from the Parson (who isn't a parson) and Sniffer Bobby and Doheny (who I haven't met yet) and Mr Breed with the funny eyes. They are almost our people and, at the moment, they seem more comfortable than him.

Robert stares at me: something behind his expression is in motion, but very slow.

'I said you don't – don't know anything. You.'

He leans on my shoulder, his mouth undecided, but his eyes fighting to focus and grow hard. 'Know everything I need.'

'Fuck you.'

'Fuck *you*.' And he slaps one foot down, beginning to barge past me and strike out for the bar.

I realise it would be weak, clinging, if I tugged him back by the sleeve, but this is what I do in any case. 'No, look, I didn't . . .' My words exhaust themselves while he shrugs himself free.

Then he halts, as if he had intended I should keep my grip. 'What? Didn't what?' The space around him starts to taste of something I don't like – of an absence, a readiness to fight. 'Tell me? Mm?' He frowns, blinks, as if he is unsure of who I am. 'You ask about *my* day? Fucking eight-year-old, bites my thumb – *bites me*. Mother – his mother – does nothing about it. I told her – *showed* her – *sleeve full of blood* – she just laughed. I wasn't even doing anything, whittling at some calculus, hardly anything – little shit bites me. *You want to wait till the hygienist gets you* – I told him – *Think I hurt? She's a fucking nightmare, grown men fucking scream, weep – choke on your own blood, that can happen*. Whispered that before he left the chair. Actually he almost fell out of it, a bit. *Skilled technician*. I am. *I care*. Fixing all these rancid bastards, do they ever say thanks? I don't have to put up with biting. I'm not paid for that.' He pauses and breathes in a mouthful of his Guinness and then forgets that he is angry. His face smoothes like a toddler's, as if he has just woken, tranquil and curious. 'So what about you?' He's beginning to grin. 'Who bit you?' At certain points in the evening, he can shift this way, like the racing of light on a breezy day. He is one man and then gone, as if you've only dreamed him.

Which means that he's not responsible for any previous offence. 'Nobody bit me. Don't be stupid.' Which can be offensive in itself. And I'd like, just now, to keep a hold of my resentment – it will stop me getting tired.

But Robert's working at me, leaning against my arm, making sure I meet at least one solid, lock-picking look, the kind that lets him nudge into my mind and change it. Not that

I won't feel better when he does.

Outside, the rain is scraping down in a solid mass, roping and marbling across the coloured glass in the windows and the smallness of the pub seems protective and intended. I would like to stay here. That'll be tricky if I'm still arguing with Robert. And this is just what his expression suggests – that we must be friends and please each other, please ourselves.

He is soothing now, as he means to be. 'What *did* they do to you? Tell Robert what they did and he will go and sort them.'

'Nobody did anything, *I* did . . .' This becomes too complicated to explain and I realise I want to slap him and I want to understand if we're going to be only friends or not – if we're going to meet here, time after time, or if we'll ever leave this tatty box full of elderly men and be somewhere else together again, alone again, the way that we were at the racetrack, in the car. Not that the car was the way I'd have wished, I can recall that it wasn't ideal, but we meant well, we did our best. Anyway, I want us to be alone together and under more suitable circumstances. Or I want to be finally sure that we never will be and able to go away and not think about him. I want him to leave me or help me. I want a clue. 'Fuck you, Robert.'

Of course, this is when he brightens and the colour in his eyes begins to deepen and turn soft. 'Oh, is *that* it?' And I can feel the slip and tumble of the lock.

Together, we raise our arms from our sides just a little to suggest that we would like to hug now, if that's okay with both of us.

Late-evening reflexes stumbling in, our hold rocks and heats and steadies and I don't know if we are both open now and freed for this, or if we've been finally caught by our touch and a mechanism has sprung shut. We may be happy or trapped, but still we blur into each other, that's what I'm sure of, what I like. We balance, unified. I kiss his mouth and miss a little, catch a tart press of fading stout and then his sweet, salt sweat. So I almost forget the way it was this morning when I held the woman on the pavement, held her, and covered myself in her blood.

Robert breathes into my hair, warming the top of my head. His shirt smells of cigarettes and future nakedness. 'Is that it? Fuck me? Fuck you? I mean . . . I mean, the last time . . .' He sounds liquid. So near to last orders, his voice is working towards one smoothed, true sound, it's singing. 'Thought youwere pissed off. After it. When we'd . . . Then. Thoughyou were pissed off withme . . . scared of you . . .'

And I'm almost the same. 'I had to throway a blouse today. My shoes. Chuck 'em.'

'Mm?' Both his hands at the small of my back, resolved and concentrating. We don't fit the bar any more, it hasn't the ambience for this. 'Youblouse . . .'

'Won't wear that suit again.'

'Quiright.' His hip shifting to ease beside the crest of mine. 'You needn't, too . . . not anything you donwant.' He frowns with solicitude and I grow teary, lick his neck. He whispers, forcing the syllables, making them carry his heat. 'So I'll take you home? Go back finish what you started? You'll ruin me, you know that . . . making me want . . . such things.'

'Someone. I threw someone out of a wheelchair today.' Whispering back with Robert's breath so near that we take each other's pace, accommodating every rise and fall. 'Threw an old lady out a wheelchair . . . when theyall came to help her I ran away.' Like this we are invisible and safe, hidden in ourselves. 'I din mean it.'

He twitches against me, then kisses my ear. 'An olady?'

'Yes.'

The twitch digs again, enquiring, 'Little olady?' And his lips tickle my cheek, knowing and playing and stealing me out of my head.

'Yes.'

We both have this tremor now between us, a problem of breath. 'A tiny, little ol . . .' The tremor worsens, jabs. And when I exhale, I discover that we are laughing, both laughing. Very, helplessly and badly and loud. 'A . . . hol lady.'

'Teeny-weeny lady.'

Although we shouldn't be happy, shouldn't even seem happy.

'Wha she do – mug you?'

Although this is awful and hurts our throats and rises up in yelps and coughs and a roaring that sways us, parts us, clatters us in.

'No. But I threw her.'

'Very far?'

And because we are dreadful and have no excuse and because I can't think about it any more, can't have it under my eyelids, or keep the sound she made stuck in my throat, or hear the wee tune she was singing – because I can't put up with it, there is nothing for me – for me and for Robert – but to howl even louder, to shout and squeal.

We are ruined by the time we lean away and see each other, we are wrecked. Robert snuffles and dunts in against my shoulder, eyes wet. 'All this . . . you know? . . . you think you can't believe it . . . sometimes . . . murder and blood and dead babies and God . . . I was telling Doheny, he was here but he's gone . . .' He wipes one cheek with the heel of his hand and sighs unevenly. 'Things like – people eat their children, people do that – God lets them – or what if my father killed my mother? Hmm? I'd be laughing the rest of my life . . .'

'Or *my* father killed *my* mother?'

'Did he? Christ, that's . . . incredibly . . . fuck, I feel nearly sober . . .'

And there is a pause here while we think that we have to go now, leave and make ourselves content. Then we kiss in a small way, this being all that we can bear, while the ache of what we will do next, must do next, hauls us straight out of the pub and across to the car which Robert threads through the shine of the downpour and the running streets until we find my flat.

Beyond that, it's a dash through the sting of rain and letting it make us new, clean, lively, and send us swinging up the stairs, feet unsure of things, but coping well in any case, all the way to my door and the usual business with keys and a shrinking lock and Robert not helping, distracting, but in the end we get inside and start the flail of coats and little arguments with buttons and glimpses of warmth and hints of skin and then both of us are simplified and clear and we do what we should have done weeks before, we do it a lot, we do it until the first birds sing the false dawn, then the real one, until Robert has to scramble out of bed, run to the car with his shirt half fastened, in a rush to be ready for morning surgery.

He accelerates away from the building with a tyre-screech that echoes in the street, earning loud and ironic applause from the flat above mine. Which is fair enough: we may very well have disturbed them – we were undoubtedly noisy enough to have woken anyone and then to have kept them sleepless the whole night. Because that's how we wanted it to be.

AUTHOR, AUTHOR

BY DAVID LODGE

The touching friendship between George Du Maurier, the fine 'Punch' illustrator and author of Victorian bestsellers, and Henry James provides the fulcrum for this outstanding novel from David Lodge. James is of course now seen as one of the great novelists of his period, a writer of enormous perception and subtlety. Lodge describes a man frustrated by his poor sales, puzzled by the huge success of his friend's book and determined to propel his career forward by writing a successful play that will relaunch him in the medium that at the time was the equivalent of both film and TV combined: the theatre.

Lodge uses both meticulous historical research and imagination to bring back to life the theatrical impresarios James dealt with including George Alexander (who put on and acted in the doomed play *Guy Domville*); the loyal servants who cherished him in London and his beloved Lamb House in Rye; and Constance Fenimore Woolson, the tragic woman who clearly loved him but with whom he could only keep a chaste and proper friendship.

David Lodge is best know for his contemporary novels and in particular those set in universities such as *Changing Places* and 'Nice Work'. Here he turns a novelist's eye on a fellow novelist and creates a completely believable portrait of a fascinating writer and fallible human being. The agony of the first night of *Guy Domville* is vividly portrayed. Instead of the acclamation he longs for (cries of "Author, Author" from the audience) the play has failed and James knows he must return

161

to his solitary life as a novelist and carry on with his unique search into the motivations of the human heart.

Author, Author succeeds superbly in making us return to the novels of Henry James enriched by this poignant and witty study of a great writer.

Recommended by Rodney Troubridge,
Waterstone's Brentford

£16.99
ISBN: 0436205270
Published September 2004

He had always been fascinated by the theatre. As young children in New York he and William were frequently taken to pantomimes, circuses and similar entertainments by their parents, who were themselves regular playgoers. One of his earliest and most vivid memories was of his mother and father going off one winter's evening from the house on Fourteenth Street to see a celebrated actress of the time, Charlotte Cushman, in *Henry VIII*, leaving himself and his brother, aged about seven and eight respectively, to do their preparation for the next day's lessons, and his father bursting into the room about an hour later, snatching up William, and rushing off with him (insofar as a man with a wooden leg, the legacy of an accident in youth, could rush) back to the theatre. The first Act had been such a sublime experience that Henry Sr. was determined his eldest son should see the rest of the performance, and had dashed home in a cab in the first interval to abduct him for that purpose. Henry, deemed too young to appreciate Shakespeare, was left alone in the lamplight with his books, bitterly resenting the deprivation. His father tried to make up for it subsequently with excursions to classic and modern plays on Broadway, but there was a sense in which no performance, in boyhood or adulthood, in New York or Paris or London, ever quite rose to the dramatic heights Henry imputed to that fabulous unseen production of *Henry VIII*. It haunted his imagination for ever after as a kind of Platonic ideal of theatrical ecstasy, which every visit to actual theatres was a vain effort to realise.

During his years in Paris he frequented the *Comédie Française* and familiarised himself with the repertoire of Scribe, Sardou and Dennery. He was a regular theatregoer in London, though its usual fare of broadly acted melodramas and farces was much inferior, in his opinion, to the productions of the Parisian stage. Indeed, it seemed to him that the English nation's besetting sin of Philistinism was nowhere more apparent than in its drama. He went night after night to sit in the stalls in the faint hope of being gripped or enchanted, and invariably returned home disappointed, sometimes before the play was over.

He happened to be in Paris, in December 1888, gratefully renewing his acquaintance with its more sophisticated style of dramatic entertainment, when he received a letter from an English actor-manager, Edward Compton, inviting him to adapt his early novel, *The American*, for the Compton Comedy Company. His first instinct was to decline. The jaunty name of the company was not promising, and he had accepted a similar proposal some ten years before, to adapt *Daisy Miller* for the New York stage, which had come to nothing. He had published the unperformed play and resolved not to waste any more time on such ventures. But on reflection he wrote a cautiously encouraging reply to Compton, and after his return to England made some enquiries of and about him, the answers to which were reassuring. Compton had a good reputation as both an actor and a manager. The repertoire of his company consisted mainly of classic English comedies by Shakespeare, Garrick, Goldsmith and the like, which they toured round the country week by week. Compton wished to enhance this programme with a new play by a prestigious writer, and to bring the production into London if it prospered. He believed that a dramatic adaptation of *The American* would fit the bill and offer rewarding parts for himself and his wife, Virginia Bateman Compton, the leading actress of the company.

The more Henry thought about this proposal – and he thought about it a good deal, sometimes when his mind should have been focused on the final chapters of *The Tragic*

Muse – the more it attracted him. By May 1889 he had agreed
in principle to write the play. More than that, he had privately
determined to write several plays – half a dozen – a dozen –
whatever it took to conquer the English stage. For all its
vulgarity and aesthetic crudity, it was for an author the
shortest road to fame and fortune – if, of course, one were
successful. But why shouldn't he succeed? He believed he had
thoroughly assimilated the craft of skilful playmaking
through years of attendance at the fountainhead of the
Française, and – heaven knew – he had sat among English
audiences long enough to know what would 'go' with them.
Compton's proposal, which he had almost dismissed out of
hand, now seemed providential, offering a solution to the
professional crisis he had confessed to Du Maurier during
their walk around the environs of Porchester Square on that
mild March evening a year before. Cushioned by moneybags
fat with playhouse royalties, he need no longer haggle with
publishers over their paltry advances, or bewail the paucity of
discriminating readers able to appreciate his novels. With the
proceeds of his commercially successful plays he would buy
himself the space and time to write real literature without
having to worry about its marketability. It was an extra
enticement that, even if the playwriting side of this projected
double career entailed some compromises with popular taste,
it would not be in itself soulless drudgery. It might even be
fun. The prospect of getting involved in the practicalities of
putting on a play, of meeting actors, attending rehearsals, and
consulting about costumes and sets, produced an undeniable
tingle of pleasurable anticipation. And then, the excitement of
seeing one's work performed in front of an audience, to hear
their laughter and applause . . . At this juncture of his
thoughts he was prone to lapse into a kind of daydream,
bathed in a golden glow of footlights, in which he himself,
immaculate in evening dress, was pulled half-resisting from
the wings of a stage amid resounding cries of 'Author!
Author!' from the auditorium, and took bow after blushing
bow.

He already knew that he must compress and divide the

action of his novel into three or four acts, with strong curtain lines; that he must exaggerate the brash 'Americanness' of his hero for the amusement of the English; and that he must contrive a happy ending to the story. In his novel the rich, self-made American Christopher Newman, an innocent abroad in Paris, was at first permitted to pay court to the beautiful young widow, the Comtesse Claire de Cintré, by her aristocratic relatives, the Bellegardes, and then snobbishly coldshouldered by them. Fate put into his hands the means of disgracing the Bellegardes or, by the threat of exposure, compelling them to allow Claire to marry him, but in a gesture of revulsion against European cynicism and corruption, Newman renounced both love and revenge and returned to his native land, while the Comtesse retired to a convent. Henry did not need Edward Compton to tell him that such a bleak conclusion would not do for a final 'note' on which to send English theatregoers home in their cabs and omnibuses and suburban trains – though Compton told him so anyway, tactfully but unequivocally, in the course of their correspondence.

For various reasons – other pressing commitments on Henry's part and a dilatoriness on Compton's that he would come to recognise as an occupational vice common to all theatrical producers – seven months passed before he actually got down to the task of adaptation. But the work went well, and the manager's comments on his drafts were encouragingly positive, though tantalisingly brief and unspecific. Curiously (as it seemed to Henry) they had never met face to face up to this point. But eventually, early in May, 1890, they made an appointment to meet in De Vere Gardens.

He awaited Compton in his large light study overlooking the street, leafing through the drafts of the play, now called *The Californian*, to refresh his memory. Tosca, the handsome dachshund bitch curled up at his feet, pricked her ears and barked, sensing the arrival of the visitor, and moments later Smith opened the door to announce: 'Mr Edward Compton and Master Compton.' Henry was surprised, and somewhat disconcerted, by the presence of the young boy, an alert, goodlooking lad aged about seven or eight, dressed in a white sailor suit, standing beside his father with a blue leatherbound book in his hand. He was also taken aback by Compton's physical appearance. A handsome, clean-shaven man in his mid-thirties, with a noble profile and a fine upright figure, he was as bald as an egg.

'I beg your pardon, Mr James,' said Compton, after they had shaken hands. 'As you see, I've taken the liberty of bringing my son with me.' He looked fondly at the boy, who was already making friends with Tosca. 'I remember what a thrill it was to me, when I was his age, to be introduced to Thackeray by *my* father – not far from here as it happens, we were walking by Kensington Gardens – and what a pleasure it was to recall that meeting in later years. I couldn't find it in me to deny him a similar privilege.'

'Of course, of course – he's most welcome!' Henry murmured, delighted by the implied compliment, though flustered by the social challenge presented by the boy. 'But how will he divert himself while we discuss our business?'

'He's under strict instructions to sit still and not interrupt,' said Edward Compton. 'But if you would be so kind as to sign his birthday book first . . .'

'Certainly, with the greatest of pleasure,' said Henry, taking the book from the boy's outstretched hand. He read the title embossed in gold on the cover. '*The Tennyson Birthday Book*. Very good. And what is your name, young man?'

'Edward Montague Compton Mackenzie,' said the boy, very clearly.

'A fine name! But how is it . . . ?' Henry wrinkled his brow in puzzlement, leaving the question unfinished.

Compton laughed. 'My own name is really Mackenzie, as was my father's. He dropped it when he went on the stage, because his Scottish relatives disapproved of the profession, and I followed suit. We usually call this young fellow "Monty".'

'I see . . . and what must I write in this fine volume, Monty?'

'Your name, if you please, sir,' said the boy. 'Under your own birthday.'

'Well, that is April the fifteenth,' said Henry, leafing through the book, which was designed like a desk diary, with a quotation from Tennyson for every day. ' " *Gorgonized me from head to foot/With a stony British stare*" – *Maud*,' he read aloud. 'Hmm. A somewhat abrasive motto for my birthday – though I know that stare. Do you know what "gorgonized" means, Monty?'

The boy blushed. 'No, sir.'

'You know about the Gorgon, Monty,' his father prompted.

'Oh the *Gorgon*,' said the boy. 'He was a monster who turned you to stone if he looked at you.'

'Very Good!' Excellent!' said Henry, impressed. 'Though I believe the creature was female.' He carried the book over to his standing desk, and wrote his name with a flourish in the appropriate place. The boy watched this operation with great curiosity.

'Do you always write standing up?' he asked.

'Monty!' his father cautioned, evidently fearing the question was impertinent.

'No,' Henry laughed. 'Sometimes I write sitting at that desk over there' – he gestured to the desk by the window covered with drafts of the play – 'and sometimes I write lying down.' He led the boy and his father over to the chaise longue, attached to which was a small lectern on a swinging arm, and demonstrated how this apparatus worked. 'I suffer from a back, you see,' he said to Compton in explanation, 'and must change my posture from time to time.'

'Very ingenious,' said Compton, admiring the swinging lectern.

'And do you hope to follow in your father's and grandfather's footsteps, Monty?' Henry asked.

'Actually, we think he might turn out to be a writer,' Compton said. 'He always has his head in a book.'

'Indeed! Then we must find you one to read now.'

Finding books for his guests to read while he was otherwise engaged was a task Henry took very seriously, aiming always for a perfect match of reader, text, and context. 'I'm afraid I don't have very much in the way of juvenile literature,' he said running his eyes anxiously along the shelves of books, pulling out an occasional volume and then replacing it with a sigh and a shake of the head. 'Andrew Lang's fairy tales are somewhat inspid I always think . . . Robert Louis Stevenson is perhaps a little advanced . . .'

'Stevenson will do admirably, Mr James,' said Compton, a little impatiently. 'I don't want to take up too much of your valuable time, and we have a play to discuss.'

'Yes, yes, of course,' said Henry, and gave young Monty *Treasure Island* to read, while they got down to business.

'I have read your fourth act,' said Compton, pulling the draft from his coat pocket.

'And approve of it, I trust?' said Henry.

'It is well written, but somewhat depressing.'

'Depressing! But it has a happy ending! The hero gets his bride.'

'Only in the last two lines. Up till then the tone is bleak and forbidding,more like a tragedy than a comedy – we *are* the Compton Comedy Company remember. The death of the brother,Valentin, casts a pall.'

They discussed this point for some time. Henry strenuously defended the death of Valentin from wounds received in a duel. The duel, with its antiquated and essentially hollow notion of 'honour', was a dramatic embodiment of the ethical difference between Europe and the New World, and the moving reconciliation of Valentin with his opponent before he expired prepared for the ultimate union of hero and heroine. Henry felt he had already sufficiently compromised the spirit of the original novel by allowing them to marry. Compton, evidently a pragmatic man, capitulated.

'Very well, but do what you can to lift the audience's spirits a bit sooner,' he said.

They went over the earlier acts and Compton made numerous suggestions for possible improvements, most of which Henry felt he could accept.

'Well, that seems to be it,' said Compton, squaring up the scattered sheets. 'I look forward to receiving a complete text

– as soon as you can. Oh – one more thing: I don't care for your new title.'

'Dear me! I thought that by making Newman a Californian – as you will remember, he's from the South in the novel – I would license myself to make his manners a little rougher, and thus more amusing in the Parisian setting,' Henry explained.

'Move him to California by all means,' said Compton, 'but keep the original title. A lot of people will come to see the play because they've read the book.'

'Really? How curious. I thought that might be a deterrent,' said Henry. Privately he had wished to suggest that the play was a new piece of work by giving it a new title, but he accepted the manager's judgement.

'Excellent,' said Compton. '"*The American*, by Henry James". It will look well on the billboards.'

'Does this mean then – am I to understand – that you are definitely going to . . .' Henry scarcely dared complete the question for fear of a negative or ambiguous answer. '*Do* it?' he finally breathed.

'Of course. Didn't I make that clear?'

'Not entirely . . . I'm delighted to hear it.'

'I'm in correspondence with your agent about terms. I'm sure there will be no difficulty.'

Henry had lately put his literary affairs in the hands of Charles Wolcott Balestier, an amiable and energetic young American who had taken up the relatively new profession of literary agent in London. Henry liked and trusted him and was delighted to have the sordid business of financial negotiations taken off his hands. 'When? And where?' were his next questions.

'We'll give the first performance at the Southport Winter Gardens, in January,' was the answer.

Henry's euphoria suffered a certain deflation. 'Not till next year?'

'We'll need all that time. There's much to be done with a new play – you'll see.'

'And why Southport? I'm not sure I even know where it is.'

'It's a seaside resort near Liverpool. A very nice place. A lot of well-off, theatregoing people live there.'

'A long way from London.'

'All the better.' Compton shot Henry a shrewd, appraising glance. 'I take it that you're interested in making money out of this play, Mr James?'

'I blush to say,' he replied, 'that it is my prime motive for venturing into this field of endeavour.'

'Well, the only way you'll make any money to speak of is with a good London run. When we tour the provinces, we spend a week in each place and put on a different play every night – so we'll only do *The American* once a week. Seat prices being what they are in the provinces, you're not going to make a fortune out of that, even if we get good houses. But in London, with stalls at half a guinea, it's a different story. A successful play could earn you a hundred pounds a week, in royalties. More.'

'Really?' Henry's eyes widened. 'So, if it ran for, say six months . . .'

'You would earn two or three thousand. Then if a play really takes, the word travels, and you get productions in America, Australia, all over. Henry Arthur Jones earned ten thousand in one year from his last play.'

'Good heavens!' Henry could almost hear the chink of sovereigns being counted in some windowless backstage office.

'But don't count your chickens before they're hatched,' said Compton, as if reading his thoughts. 'London audiences are hard to please, and the competition is fierce. That's why I want to work on this play in the provinces – give it a good airing on tour – see how it goes with audiences – get everything right before we bring it to London. You understand me?'

'I do, and am much obliged to you for the explanation,' said Henry.

'Southport is a good place to start. As a matter of fact the Winter Gardens was the very first venue the company played. It's always been a lucky house for me. Theatre folk are somewhat superstitious about such things. Have you any other questions, Mr James, before I go?'

171

Henry had another question, but didn't quite know how to put it. Compton however, perceived the import of his involuntary upward glance.

'Yes,' he said, smiling. 'I shall wear a toupee for the part of Newman.'

'I presumed so,' said Henry, but he was relieved to hear it.

In September Henry went to Sheffield, where the company was performing its current repertory at the Theatre Royal, to read his finished play to the assembled actors. Compton was at the station to meet him and conduct him to his hotel. Henry had never been to Sheffield before, knowing it only as a name stamped on cutlery, and was surprised to find how extensive it was, a city of grey stone and rusting iron, sprawled over the Yorkshire hills in the slanting late afternoon sunshine, with soot-blackened steeples, fuming factory chimneys, noisy bustling streets – and a theatre. The next morning he sat on its stage on a hard upright chair, with his back to the darkened auditorium, and the cast, similarly seated, facing him in a semicircle, and read the play straight through, with only brief pauses between the acts. He threw himself energetically into the task, drawing on such histrionic skills as he had acquired in the charades at New Grove House, and similar party games in his New England youth. He knew it was important to enthuse the actors with the parts they would be playing, and it was also an invaluable opportunity to indicate how his lines should be spoken, for he was by no means confident of Compton's American accent, or the other actors' ability to impersonate French aristocrats. He had no idea what the protocol was on such an occasion, or what kind of response to expect from his little audience. They seemed to enjoy the first act, smiling and laughing aloud on occasion, but as the play went on they grew silent. The play itself of course became more sombre as it progressed, and that was no doubt the reason. When he finished, exhausted and hoarse from the effort, there was a patter of applause, and polite smiles and murmured thankyous from the actors, but they jumped up from their seats and disappeared with disconcerting speed.

'Where has everybody gone?' Henry wondered aloud as Compton helped him on with his overcoat.

'They have gone for their dinners,' said Compton, 'and I think we should go for ours. Mrs Compton is waiting for us.' Mrs Compton, who was to play Claire Cintré, had excused herself from attending the reading as she was already thoroughly familiar with the play from the various drafts Henry had sent. The manager led Henry out of the theatre and they walked side by side along the London Road.

'The road to London – a good omen,' Henry quipped.

'I hope so,' said Compton expressionlessly.

Henry waited for further comment, but none was forthcoming.

'So, what is your first – what is your immediate impression, my dear Compton?' he asked.

'The play is too long,' said the manager.

'Too long?' Henry exclaimed, genuinely surprised. 'You didn't say so when we met in May.'

'You have added a great deal since then,' said Compton grimly, striding on.

'Well, perhaps a line here and there . . .' said Henry.

'Much more than that. I told you the play should occupy two hours and three quarters, including the entr'actes.' Compton took out his fob watch from under the lapels of his topcoat, and examined it. 'You started reading at eleven o'clock this morning. You finished at about three. That's four hours.'

'But I read all the stage directions as well,' he pleaded in mitigation.

'Those actions have to be performed. It all takes time. Add the entr'actes, and if we begin this play at seven, it will be nearly midnight before the final curtain comes down. Quite impossible.'

'But what is to be done?' Henry cried.

'We must cut it,' said Compton.

Henry came to an abrupt stop in the middle of the pavement under the shock of this suggestion. He had laboured for weeks, weighing and polishing every line like a jeweller with his gems, to create a seamless glittering necklace of words. The idea of this beautiful artefact being hacked into an abbreviated form was like the plunge of a sharp instrument into his own flesh. '*Cut* it? How?'

'With a blue pencil.' Compton grinned, somewhat heartlessly Henry thought. 'There was never a play written that didn't benefit from cutting. My wife is very good at it.'

There commenced a very painful period of two months during which Henry was gradually compelled by the polite but implacable Comptons to surrender about a quarter of his precious lines.

The process was carried on mainly by letter and telegram. Henry's expenditure on telegrams rose alarmingly, and threatened to consume a significant proportion of the advance of £250 that Balestier had negotiated for him. This medium of communication, though undoubtedly convenient, always confronted Henry with an agonising conflict between considerations of economy on the one hand and literary elegance on the other. Straining to reconcile these two desiderata he produced telegraphic communications that had at times something of the quality of a Japanese haiku, like: 'WILL ALIGHT PRECIPITATELY AT 5.38 FROM THE DELIBERATE 1.50. HENRY JAMES.' When professional matters were involved the thought of economising on the length of the message, sacrificing nuances of meaning to save a coin or two, did not even arise; and it often cost him a hundred telegraphed words to defend the retention of a single phrase in his play, which in the end he was obliged, more often than not, to discard. It was a miserable and frustrating business, but he persevered, reminding himself all the while that this was how he was going to liberate himself from the chains of financial anxiety. And there was after all a kind of grim satisfaction to be obtained from wrestling successfully with the arbitrary constraints of theatrical convention and the stubborn prejudices of actor-managers.

*

On the afternoon of Saturday the 3rd of January 1891, with only hours to go before the first public performance of *The American*, Henry paced up and down his sitting room in the Prince of Wales Hotel, Southport, belching and breaking wind intermittently. He had declined Compton's invitation to share the dinner the manager always took punctually at three o'clock when he was performing in the evening, and ordered a cold collation in his room, but perhaps this had been a mistake. A hot meal would have been more calming to bowels churning with anxiety. He summoned the waiter to remove the soiled dishes, and sat down at the table to write some letters – rather like a soldier, it occurred to him, on the eve of a battle which he might not survive.

The dress rehearsal of the previous day had confirmed his opinion that the play would stand or fall by its intrinsic qualities, for the acting was mostly pedestrian and the stage settings minimal (though it was an undoubted enhancement to see Compton with a toupee covering his bald pate at last, and a moustache on his upper lip for good measure). Henry had tried to watch the play as if it were the work of another hand, and it seemed to him that it did hang together and move along at an exemplary pace. But it was hard to judge with only a thin scattering of auditors, mostly employees of the theatre and their relations, in the cavernous theatre. All fifteen hundred seats were sold for tonight, and he would have to sit among the occupants and register their verdict. One of them would be William Archer, the influential critic of *The World*, who had written to Henry welcoming the prospect of a new play by a distinguished man of letters, and announcing his intention of attending the premiere. Henry was both flattered and alarmed by this message. Archer had something of a mission to raise the literary standards of the English stage, an aim with which Henry had every sympathy, but he was a fervent supporter of Ibsen, about whom Henry had reservations, and he could be a harsh critic of work that displeased him.

To kill time Henry put on his overcoat and went out to post his letters himself, instead of giving them to the hotel reception desk, where he paused however to bespeak a late supper for himself, the Comptons, and Balestier, who was on his way from London by train. The meal would be either a celebration or a wake. After calling at the Post Office, he strolled along the marine promenade. There were few people about on this cold winter afternoon. The tide was out, far, far out, and the sun, largely obscured by cloud, was setting over the flat wet sand and an almost invisible sea. An inordinately long skeletal pier stretched from the shore towards the horizon, as if it had set off to bridge the Irish Sea and lost heart. It seemed absurd that he, Henry James, the 'distinguished man of letters', the cosmopolitan author equally at home in London, Paris, Rome and New York, should have fetched up here in the middle of winter, in this flat and featureless provincial resort, on the very rim of civilisation as it seemed, anxiously to await the determination of his fate as an aspirant playwright. At the thought he gave a loud, barking guffaw of self-mocking laughter, which caused a gentleman passing by to look at him sharply and disapprovingly, obviously under the impression that he was drunk.

Henry went on to the theatre. The man in the little cubby hole by the stage door recognised him. 'There's nobody in from the company, Mr James. They're all having a rest this afternoon.'

'I know,' said Henry. 'Thank you. I merely wish to reassure myself about some details of the set.'

He mooned around the stage for some time, fiddling with the props for the first scene, 'A Parisian Parlour', by the dim illumination of a single gaslight, and adjusting the placing of the chairs by an inch or two. The curtain was down for some reason. On an impulse he parted the two flaps, stepped out in front of the curtain, and looked into the enormous maw of the dark, empty auditorium. He waited a few moments till his eyes accommodated to the gloom and he was quite sure he was alone. Then, gravely and deliberately, he practised a bow.

If it was an act of hubris, it went unpunished. A few hours later he stood in the same spot, dazzled by footlights, bowing with the applause of fifteen hundred spectators roaring in his ears. The ovation was loud and long – long enough to warrant three bows. The beaming Compton, who had already taken several himself, seized Henry's hand in both of his own and shook it vigorously. His lips formed the word 'Congratulations!' Then the curtain came down for the last time, and the applause died away into a buzz of animated conversation as the audience filed out of the theatre.

Compton turned to the actors.'Well done, ladies and gentlemen,' he said.

'Yes, indeed, you were all wonderful.Wonderful!' Henry seconded, going round shaking their hands. He had a special word of thanks for Mrs Compton, whose hand he kissed in homage. The actors dispersed to their dressing rooms with pleased smiles. Henry and Compton followed them into the wings.'It seemed to go very well,' Henry said, with affected casualness.

'Well? It was a triumph.'

'Do you really think so?'

'Absolutely.'

'You were magnificent, my dear Compton,' Henry said, and he spoke sincerely. The manager's performance had been a revelation. Nothing he had seen in rehearsal had prepared him for its passion and energy.

'Having an audience makes all the difference.'

'Indeed it does,' said Henry. Being part of it that evening, watching his own play through its ears and eyes, had been an extraordinary experience, as if the big black maw of the auditorium which he had looked into that afternoon had swallowed him and, like Jonah in the whale, he was both part of this great live breathing creature and yet distinct from it. He felt every tremor and vibration of its reaction to the spectacle on the stage, he registered the strength of every collective laugh and chuckle, and measured the intensity of every silence at moments of dramatic tension, while himself remaining strangely detached, unmoved and unamused by the familiar material. It was such a novel sensation that at first he distrusted the evidence of success. In the interval at the end of the first act he hastened backstage and buttonholed Compton in the wings. 'In heaven's name,' he said, 'tell me. Is it *going*?' 'Going? Rather!' had been the reassuring reply. 'You could hear a pin drop.' And to judge by the reception at the end, the other three acts had 'gone' just as well.

Balestier came up, his fresh eager face nodding enthusiastically atop his long, thin, wandlike frame, and wrung Henry's hand.

'Congratulations, my dear chap, we have a hit on our hands,' he said.

'Do you really think so?' Henry said.

'Ask this man,' Balestier said, nodding at Compton.

'I've already told him,' said Compton. 'And it will be even better by the time we get to London.'

Henry left them talking, and hastened back to the hotel to order champagne to be served with the supper. He floated along the street in a kind of bubble of euphoria, which survived a slightly prickly encounter shortly afterwards with William Archer. He was surprised, while supervising the laying of the table in his sitting room at the hotel, to receive the critic's card, but invited him to come up. He struck Henry as surprisingly young, somewhat resembling a Nonconformist minister in appearance and manners.

'I see you are preparing for a party,' he said, looking rather disapprovingly at the champagne bottles cooling in ice buckets. 'I will not detain you long. I thought I would give you the benefit of my first impressions of your play. I could not find an opportune moment at the theatre.'

'It's very kind of you,' said Henry politely, though he would willingly have postponed the pleasure.

Archer proceeded to make some detailed criticisms of the play's construction, which Henry hardly had the patience to follow.There would be a time for tinkering and polishing later. Now he wanted to gorge on his success. 'You will grant, I think, that the play was very well received tonight,' he said, with a touch of asperity.

'Indeed. But it is the kind of play that goes better in the provinces than in London,' said Archer. Shortly after delivering this opinion, he took his leave.

Henry's spirits were slightly dashed by the encounter, but soon afterwards the Comptons and Balestier arrived in buoyant mood, and after a glass or two of champagne the bubble of euphoria enclosed him again. They ate their supper with leisurely relish as they reviewed the many high points of the evening, like soldiers lolling in their tent, reliving a victorious battle. It was nearly two o'clock in the morning when the happy party broke up. Before he retired to bed, Henry drafted a telegram to be sent to Alice first thing the next morning, as he had promised his sister. For once, a not strictly grammatical stream of words and phrases seemed rhetorically justified. He wrote: 'UNQUALIFIED TRIUMPHANT MAGNIFICENT SUCCESS UNIVERSAL CONGRATULATIONS GREAT OVATION FOR AUTHOR GREAT FUTURE FOR PLAY COMPTONS RADIANT AND HIS ACTING ADMIRABLE WRITING HENRY.' It summed up his feelings about the evening perfectly.

SPANISH STEPS

BY TIM MOORE

Tim Moore's first travelogue, *Frost on My Moustache*, was published in 1999 to some acclaim. Self-effacingly labelling himself a "loafer" – although what kind of loafer embarks on a journey to the Arctic I'm not really sure – Moore subsequently tackled the Monopoly Board in a London odyssey (*Do Not Pass Go*) and cycled the route of the Tour de France in 'French Revolutions'. *Spanish Steps* is the story of another epic adventure, this time on an ancient pilgrim trail across Spain, heading towards Santiago de Compostela. Following in the footsteps of Saint James, Paolo Coelho and... Shirley MacLaine, Moore's bright idea to really emulate the pilgrim experience is to bring along a donkey for the journey, although in truth this has little to do with historical authenticity: "Buggered if I'm carrying a rucksack".

Predictably, this is not a plan that turns out quite as happily as the author would have liked. Saddled with a recalcitrant Pyrenean ass named Shinto, Moore finds himself faced with a 750-kilometre journey with a creature that refuses to cross bridges and is intent on stopping to eat vast swathes of the Spanish countryside at any opportunity. Moore's initial hair-tearing despair at his travelling companion's bloody-mindedness is dryly and wittily evoked, in a way that suggests the memories are still horribly fresh in his mind: "I'd experience the starkest difficulties on the more challenging inclines and descents, and on this basis it was a shame that my first task was to get Shinto up the Pyrenees and . . . straight back down again."

Meeting many a pilgrim along the way, and often interrupting his narrative for a flippant observation about Spanish history, *Spanish Steps* is the hugely entertaining tale of an ultimately moving journey, which fans of Bill Bryson and Dave Gorman will relish.

Recommended by Owen Williams,
Waterstone's Bristol University

£16.99
ISBN: 0224062654
Published August 2004

Comfortably more convenient than pilgrimage rivals Rome and Jerusalem, Santiago was always the British holy traveler's preferred destination. Shakespeare included references to 'cockle hats and staffs' in *Hamlet* and Sir Walter Ralegh even composed a rhyming eulogy to the pilgrimage. 'Give me my scallop-shell of quiet, My staff of faith to walk upon . . . My gown of glory, hope's true gage, And thus I'll take my pilgrimage,' he wrote, and though he actually never did, skeletons clad in decayed pilgrim cloaks and clutching scallop shells to their ribs have been uncovered in church crypts throughout the land.

The eleventh-century British vanguard came on pray-and-slay crusades to take on the Moors; later, we helped pioneer pilgro-tourism and so, say I, inaugurated a long tradition of holidaying in Spain (and as souvenirs go, it's tough to top remission of accumulated sins). We stayed loyal to Santiago even as the ever shifting allegiances of medieval Europe threw up new hazards: British pilgrim ships were regularly held to ransom in Spanish ports, and in 1375 six pilgrims from Yorkshire were executed as traitors on their return from Santiago, unaware that they had passed through Castille during a period of alliance with the hated French.

No one is certain how many Brits travelled overland, but good records exist of those who took the pilgrim ferries direct to Spain – William Wey, the most notable British pilgrim chronicler, sailed from Plymouth to La Coruña ('La Groyne' in his unfortunate translation) in an impressive four days.

Even in the fifteenth century, with the pilgrimage's popularity well past its peak, over 3,000 pilgrims were voyaging from Britain every year.

But even when Anglo-French relations sank to their murderous worst, there were always those for whom the express sea route was a little lightweight, a little inauthentic. To walk, it was said, was to pray with one's feet. And for those, as I discovered between the forbidding covers of *Jacobean Pilgrims from England to St James from the Early Twelfth to the Late Fifteenth Century*, a regularly favoured stopover was at any of the friendly monasteries of southern France, where many – oh, happy, happy words – 'were given or lent an ass for the journey'.

I'd found Hanno after a desperate request to Jan and Nick Flanagan, at whose cycling-based lodging house Pyrenean Pursuits I had been a guest some years before. I needed a donkey, I needed him in or near Spain, and with the summer pilgrim rush I'd been urged to avoid now encroaching, I needed him fast. Hanno, I should perhaps point out, was not a donkey. He was very much a man, indeed a vital, bearded Hagrid of a man who hurled my belongings into the dusted rear of his much-travelled Landcruiser with a single swing of a long arm. The Continental donkey enthusiast was evidently a breed apart from his pigtailed Sidmouth counterpart.

Apprehensive as to how I might recognise my donk vendor when he arrived to meet me at a bedrizzled Carcassonne airport, Hanno had described himself as having 'much disorder in the hair'. As long as this hadn't seeped into the head below I didn't mind. For two weeks I'd been in constant, if indirect, contact with Mañuel Bazquez, a man tracked down by a Spanish-resident friend of mine, John Perring. The service Mañuel provided seemed ideal for my needs: he hired donkeys to Spanish pilgrims, providing all the medical kit and saddle-bags and so on, and after a month drove all the way to Santiago to pick them up in a horse trailer. A one-way rental, and for only 600 euros all in.

There were a couple of drawbacks. One was that I'd never

manage 774 kilometres in a month. Another was that Mañuel didn't have any donkeys.

I'm not sure why it took Mañuel so long – a dozen emails and as many phone calls – to divulge this important fact to John, but his failure to do so didn't augur well for future dealings with the tradesmen of Spain. On day one Mañuel had fourteen donkeys, but by day eight a party of pilgrims had led half of those away. Then on day twelve, without explanation, a solitary jackass browsed Mañuel's yard. 'We've got to make him an offer on that one pronto,' I told John.

'Absolutely right.'

Twelve hours later John phoned me back. 'He's just sold it to a shepherd.'

A day of silence was followed by an email of blurted self-castigation, in which Mañuel confessed that his rental business was no longer an active one; that indeed it was now – put the chisel down, Mr Moore – *two years* since last a bray had been heard in his grounds. 'People who rented his donkeys couldn't cope,' elaborated John that evening as I held the receiver to my limp and sallow features, 'especially when it rained a lot. They just abandoned them by the road.'

I can't say this was a happy time. Mañuel's customers had been Spanish, and so by definition more culturally at ease with donkeys: so at ease that when they weren't weaving toy examples together out of raffia to flog to unsophisticated foreigners, they were lugging real ones up the church tower and heaving them off as a fiesta ice-breaker.

As we rumbled and roared through damp villages, I waited for Hanno to explain in his proficient English why I had nothing to fear. Instead I learnt that people would think I was a *gitano*, or gypsy, and would consequently drive the donkey off their land, to be met by real *gitanos*, or gypsies, who would steal it. I learnt how I'd need to treat the animal for ticks every three weeks, and then in dramatic terms how to effect this by jabbing a stout hypodermic through its breast – an enactment that required him to remove both hands from the steering-wheel whilst overtaking a tractor.

'You are strong?'

Hanno glanced at my T-shirt and what it contained, saving us both the discomfort of a verbal reply. 'But you will be. You must be. In the first days the *donkay* must understand that you are the boss. You will be . . . *physical* to him.'

Walking a donkey on asphalt, as following the camino would regularly require me to, dangerously eroded its hoofs; better to take a compass and just head off cross-country, snipping barbed fences with wire-cutters. I should also be wary of crypto-fascists, two-faced priests and snakes. 'Be very careful, huh?' he warned at the end of almost every sentence, rather superfluously for what had now been upgraded from a culturo–spiritual voyage of discovery to a fatally ill-equipped commando raid by the *Dad's Army* cavalry.

Tarmac turned to mud and we bumped up, across and then down a mist-wreathed hillside. The sudden violence of our progress seemed to dislodge a rogue nugget of inner defiance: what did he know, anyway? Panoramane, Hanno's one-man ass-for-hire operation, rented donkeys for cosy three- and four-day hikes around the foothills of the French Pyrenees. Long-distance travel was not his business, and nor was anything Spanish. By his own admission he'd never even sold a donkey before.

Despite this stage of the journey causing his considerable head to impact repeatedly against the cab roof, the proximity of home seemed to mellow Hanno. 'But what you are doing, it's a . . . a very *strong* experience.' He kissed the bunched fingertips of his right hand. 'You will find again the, ah, ancient rhythms of life, a *nomade* with another *nomade* at your side.' We rumbled down a muddy hairpin and up to a wooden house in the latter stages of construction; he killed the engine. 'Possessions will have no meaning,' continued Hanno, his glassy gaze on the bedrizzled valley below, perhaps willing me to imagine no religion.

'*Voilà.*' An asinine honk blared out, and there, trotting down through the tussocked greenery, were a dozen damp donks. Big donks: wildly shaggy, almost bison-like in their brunette sturdiness. Feeling like a motorist whose car has broken down in a safari park, I managed a mechanical wave.

'Which one is mine?' I asked, unable to keep a quaver out of my voice.

Hanno scanned the long, dark faces. 'He's not here at this moment. Sometimes you find him, ah . . .' Bleeding? Foaming? Sinking? Hanging? '. . . Hiding.'

'So, um, how do you know?' I enquired as Hanno climbed into the back to pass me the bags out under the gormless scrutiny of his herd, mercifully coralled behind an electric fence.

'Hmm?'

'About, you know, the experience. And its strength.'

Boldly oblivious to the constraints of his surroundings, Hanno depicted incredulity with the very Frenchest of all body gestures. 'But I have done it!'

All we'd established in the first of our two brief calls was that he had a spare donkey, and would sell it to me for 800 euros. The second had covered logistical arrangements.

'But you knew, no? Five year ago I walk from Belgium to Santiago with my family and two donkays.'

It was him! And he wasn't even French! This was quite something. 'Why will I sell you donkay if not for this reason? I don't sell donkays, but this adventure you make, it's special, and so I like to help.'

Following Hanno up into his home I felt as if I was being inducted into a benign secret society. Within lay yet more evidence that the people who did this pilgrimage were clearly not as I was. No television, but a computer monitor with a donkey-themed screen saver. A wood-burning stove and a supper-cooking wife, the welcoming, winsome Marie-Christine, chopping home-grown vegetables at a long, slender table. The more youthful of their two daughters breezed about in a headscarf. Her elder sister, evidently at a more challenging stage of young adulthood, had by mutual request been installed in the guest room. This was an old caravan 100 yards uphill, yet still her parents found themselves within the radius of adolescent loathing: asked to find alternative accommodation with friends for the two days of my visit, she had apparently almost smiled.

We dined by congenial candlelight, Hanno divulging relevant facts as they occurred to him. I'd brought a voice recorder along, and pushed it next to his plate as he listed and described more poisonous plants, and the importance of feeding a donkey – in fact my donkey, wherever he was – a handful of rock-salt every morning, and the need to find shelter if the rain lasted more than two days. He talked of the time a Spanish farmer kidnapped his donkeys in the night and held them for ransom. Had he mentioned the snakes? He had. And the thieves? Well, some of them. *'Oh, c'est pas comme ça,'* tutted Marie-Christine at the end of almost every one of his more lurid stories. But every time she did he raised a bushy eyebrow the short distance to his tangled fringe and smiled knowingly.

Postprandially spread-eagled in an ancient, low-slung armchair with his booted feet steaming against the stove door, Hanno described how the walk to Santiago had changed his life. Seven months it had taken, requiring him to take his two daughters – then six and nine – out of school for a year. Romany meandering by day; maths and French round the evening camp-fire. Upon return, his inner nomad out of the box and restless, Hanno flogged the family home and moved down here; a portraitist of startling talent, he now earned his crust depicting from photographs the children of Belgium's aristocrats and industrialists. For him this had become a mechanical chore, but by spreading that crust with donkeys he had made himself an improbably toothsome life sandwich. Drawing children gave this irrepressible trend-bucker the freedom to indulge his passion for hosing crap out of a big shed. In another year Hanno and Marie-Christine, this time alone, would be heading off again, circumnavigating the Iberian peninsula with the same two donkeys.

Outside it was black and wet. En route to the caravan Hanno and I were joined by two lumbering, long-haired dogs; mindful of the looming festival of contrived hearty petting, I treated the fatter to a couple of manly slaps. Hanno led me through the slick grass towards the first of the electric fences: 'With care here,' he warned as his torch picked out the first electric fence. 'One time I touch with my head and my mouth is frozen for twelve hour.'

'But I thought these were just run off car batteries. 12 volts?'

'Sometimes, but here is too many fences. I put it on the, ah, real *electricité*.'

'What, 240 volts?'

He recoiled in bafflement. '*Non, 22,000.*'

I looked at him, my mouth pre-frozen.

'But with small watts.'

Once past this appalling forcefield, our menagerie was unsettlingly complemented by half a dozen silhouetted equines. 'They're all *men*,' I said, playing a torch across their under-sides as Hanno fumbled for the caravan key. Almost universal advice to source a more placid and willable female ass coloured my voice with a disappointment that he handsomely failed to detect. 'Yes,' he said, gurning lewdly at a wrist-thick parabola of swarthy love muscle. 'We have an expression – *monté comme un âne.*' Hanno inhaled loudly and expressed his comic awe with that burnt-my-fingers shake of the hand. 'You know – mounted as a donkay.'

'Yes, we say something a bit like that.'

'My donkays are all, ah, cut, but they still enjoy to cover the ladies. Eh! Here is your one.'

And so I first beheld my ass. Blinking into Hanno's torch beam he shuffled up through the trees, then idled circumspectly in the background as his fieldmates jostled and stamped and nuzzled steam at my throat. As they were dark so he was mousy; as they were loudly tousled so he was neat and petite. Tiny and tawny. Low-key, reticent: My Little Donkey amongst the rodeo rowdies, Charlie Watts at the back of a stage full of posturing Jaggers.

'Eh, Shinto!'

I'd been thinking about a name for two weeks; on the plane the choices had been distilled to a toss-up between Doug and Judas. But now it was Shinto, and as he perked up his browny-grey ears at its bellowed enunciation, I knew that however inappropriate it seemed to travel a hallowed

Catholic trail with a beast named after a polytheistic Oriental religion, I couldn't change it.

Shinto looked me in the eyes, blinked once more, then sauntered off into the night. 'He is the most intelligent of all my donkays, and the least nervous.' An appealing claim, whose relative nature did not at this stage occur to me.

The caravan was pertinently monastic – clean but spartan. Before he left Hanno shone his beam at its plumbed facilities, a few yards downhill in a log cabin of his own design and construction, solar-heated shower and all. (Though as I'd later discover to my nocturnal disadvantage, he'd cut a few corners on the toilet: a plastic dustbin and an adjacent bag of sawdust, a bran tub I'd be stocking with mystery prizes for two days.) The donkeys parted for him, and now I was alone. Alone in a caravan cornered by donkey shit and high voltage, yet if the accounts I'd read of the pilgrim *refugios* were to be believed, this was as good as it would get for the next 774 kilometres.

I listened to the tape I'd made at dinner as mountain rain shotblasted the thin roof. Even amidst the racket I could detect in Hanno's tone a slight incredulity – he evidently hadn't believed I was quite as useless as I'd insisted I was. 'You don't know the different type of straw, not at all?' 'The chair or bowline knot you can do, of course. No? Really, no?'

The tape clicked off, and as I yanked the paisley curtains together a herd of rustling shadows swished into the trees. Now was not the moment to recall Hanno's tale of the time he'd borrowed a lady donk, a jenny, for breeding purposes: his boys had all had her up against the caravan, and in the process knocked it over. As I pondered this, a mighty, awful bray banged off down the valleys – no more apocalyptic by day than the hearty priming of an ancient hand pump, that night, alone in the caravan, it was the rusted gates of hell being effortfully forced ajar.

Throughout the long hours of darkness I was unsettled visibly – and on one unhappy occasion audibly – by extraneous asinine activity. As dawn fingered in round the curtains I felt like rushing down to the house and shaking Hanno by his huge shoulders: It's all right for you, mate, you build solar showers and train your own donkeys and . . . and . . . and I just can't do this. Because I didn't even have to. You didn't need a donkey to take a Ryanair baggage allowance across Spain. Nineteen kilos on the nose – dump a couple of books, and whatever I'd said before, I could shoulder that. Or I could . . . get on the next plane back to London.

At breakfast the phone ruptured a sombre silence. Marie-Christine handed me the receiver: it was Birna, reporting in fretful distress that the children's scalps were alive with lice, and that the plumber had just found a rat behind the boiler. Someone didn't want me to give up and go home. Our Mister was already working in mysterious ways.

I followed Hanno out into the paddock, and looking around began to feel better. The rain had gone and under a big blue sky I saw what the Pyrenees had that Belgium didn't. Densely medieval forests pitched and rolled, surrendering at distant length to fearsome snow-veined peaks: here were the Himalayan foothills transplanted to Somerset on a perfect morning in the butterfly season. Walking from Italy or central France, a medieval pilgrim would typically bank on getting to Santiago and back in four months; those setting out from Britain or the more distant central European lands might allow a year, over-wintering in Spain before heading home. Either way, spring was the time to set out if you wanted to avoid that chilly short cut to paradise on some snowbound Pyrenean peak. Chaucer noted that no month aroused wanderlust more powerfully than April, and though he was talking about an English April, or rather Aprille, contemplating the panorama I saw what he meant.

At least until that panorama had donkeys in it. Albeit largely in the background, for despite Hanno's beckoning clucks and whistles the bulk of his herd – though happily not Shinto – just gawped blankly at us from a great distance. Here was a man who bred and rented donkeys, who had walked halfway down Europe with donkeys, and still they sometimes ignored him, sometimes slipped his knots and got lost in the night, sometimes bit him. 'They bite? What do you do then?' We were outside the stable now, being jostled by over-familiar quadrupeds.

'Oh, a bite is not so serious. But if he kick you – then you must attack with your hands.' He thrust out a taut fist; I began to explain that this wasn't quite the pilgrim ethos I'd had in mind. Was that really how Jesus prepared for his Palm Sunday ride into Jerusalem? 'Of course! You cannot train a donkay without pain! When he kick, you hit him with power in the stomach.' With disquieting relish he thus punished an imaginary animal. '*Bof!* Always in the stomach. Their pain centre.'

Shinto? Kung fu more like. I pictured a trio of stubbled apostles – perhaps St James himself among them – pinning down a disobedient jackass while their grim-faced messiah systematically worked him over. I remembered my grim encounter with a full edition of Robert Louis Stevenson's donkey journal: 'I must reach the lake before sundown, and to have even a hope of this must instantly maltreat this uncomplaining animal. The sound of my own blows sickened me.' And I found myself recalling how a friend's father had once had a fight – a proper fists-and-feet brawl – with a pony who'd thrown off one of his daughters. Did it really have to be this way?

Shinto's associates wandered away and we were left with a rather circumspect grey animal. By the end of a long night I'd become rather good at blotting out the brooding enormity of what lay ahead, and watched in gone-past-caring non-chalance as Hanno lashed the toughened plastic packsaddle to Shinto's back by means of a fiendish cat's cradle of straps and buckles. 'Ah, this strap here to the behind, have it low so he don't *caca* on it.' He threw me the head collar and watched as I confidently attached it in a new way, a way that pinned Shinto's left ear to his neck. Wordlessly Hanno put this right, and we were off, taking my new donk for a test drive.

My mentor took the reins, lightly holding the five-foot-long red-and-green leading rope in finger and thumb and position-ing himself just behind Shinto. 'Eeeeeuuuwwwww,' he groaned, like a one-man football crowd bemoaning a near miss. It wasn't a noise I'd anticipated, but before it was even halfway out of his throat Shinto broke into a brisk trot that had us jogging up the forest path behind him.

Five minutes on Hanno handed me the rope, along with a pliable length of willow, and trying to gloss over the momentousness I took my place at Shinto's rear. 'Eeeeeuuuwwww,' I said, or tried to. It would be a lie to say Shinto didn't move, because one of his ears swivelled back. 'Eeeeeuuuwwww!' Nothing. Hanno stood in front, looking at me like a driving instructor watching a new student put the ignition key in his own ear and twist. He took a step back towards us, half a step really, and Shinto immediately jolted into motion.

Hanno never had to say anything twice to Shinto, but with me even that was never enough. Repetition lent his more despairing exhortations the familiarity of a catchphrase. 'It is a problem of *autorité,*' was one. 'So once more – *why a* donkay?' was another. 'You are not so convincing' – his favourite – was typically accompanied with a palsied shake of the wrist that paralleled my attempts at physical chastisement to an incredibly old woman trying to coax ink from a reluctant Biro. 'Don't make my donkay too English,' said Hanno after one such episode. '"Oh, please, Mr Shinto,"' he went on, his voice ascending to a prissily camp facsimile of a flustered public schoolboy from the inter-war years, '"Would you care to advance a little faster?"'

'He's not your donkey now,' I said, letting my willow fall to the soft earth.

At my persistent and desperate behest Shinto eventually moved forward, with the eager brio of a hill start effected in third gear. We toiled up through an empty village, and onwards to an open escarpment girdled majestically by muscular peaks. It was hot. Hanno threw his leather jacket over Shinto's saddle and sparked up a Marlboro. 'There is Spain, there,' he said, jabbing its lit end at the southern horizon. And then we headed back down.

Shinto quickly took stock of this new approach to gradient, and used it to develop momentum. For perhaps five of my steps and ten of his we were in the zone, striding purposefully as one. Then the footpath steepened and in moments he was hurtling crazily down its sun-dappled hairpins; I grabbed the rope in both hands and was pulled helplessly along like a novice waterskier. Hanno's jacket flew from saddle to nettles, but before stopping to retrieve it he distantly crooned out a noise that sounded like his 'Eeeeeuuuwwww' played backwards. Shinto slammed on the anchors and I slid groin first into his rump.

'When you go up,' panted Hanno as he rejoined us, 'you stand behind with your *baton*. But when you go down, you must be ahead, and hold the *baton* in front of his eyes. As a brake?' He snapped a leafy switch from an adjacent birch and handed it to me, not unfriendly but with determination. Nodding wordlessly, I wiped the back of a wrist against my humid brow. Getting Shinto to move had appeared to be the significant problem; now I understood the more fundamental disadvantages of not getting him to stop. If he decided to go, he was gone: unless I mastered that noise or got hold of a stun gun, there was nothing to be done. Shinto stood there, motionless and four-square, like an eighteenth-century livestock portrait. Shakily I raised the branch to his face. He gazed through its resident foliage for a moment, then with a sudden snatch of the jaw broke the stick off about three inches from my fingers and settled into its protracted consumption.

'You have too much *fatalisme*,' said Hanno as he led Shinto up the rutted drive to his German friend Mikkael's house. I said nothing. The almost constant reiteration of my ignorance and incompetence was coagulating doubt into a clot of raw fear, a mass that having filled my stomach was now pressing painfully into the diaphragm. I tried telling myself that this was precisely the sort of feeble unmanliness I'd come to confront, but then if Hanno's assessment of my character really was accurate – which of course it was – then why be a pilgrim? Just as fatalism dictates that nothing a man does can alter his destiny, so a pilgrimage was predicated on the precise opposite. The options for the weeks and months ahead were hardening: philosophical overhaul of the starkest profundity, or stupid, craven, self-fulfilling shambles.

Mikkael was a retired professor with two donkeys and a cottage he rented out in the summer. During our brief stay Shinto damaged all three. As we ate salami and yoghurt on an overwhelmingly panoramic terrace, Shinto contrived a confrontation with his new equine associates that had them all flailing about in a limb-knotted cartoon brawl. Chastised, and with a red-crescent bite on his neck, he then trotted up to the immaculate gardens fronting Mikkael's cottage and lowered his big snout purposefully into a flower-bed.

We could see his jaw working, and I was the nearest. 'Tim, maybe you, ah . . .' said Hanno. And so I, ah, did, quickly finding myself in a ridiculous Mexican stand-off, meeting a gaze that if not quite withering, was unsettlingly implacable. Eating flowers might be fun, but how much more fun to stare out this silly new man. I looked hard into those eyes, round and shiny as freshly shelled conkers, and beheld the very essence of dumb insolence. Then Hanno appeared at my shoulder and he trotted smartly to heel.

Marie-Christine contemplated our belated return from their stilt-propped veranda. I saw her whilst urging a static Shinto towards his field with a nervously jabbed forefinger in the haunch, like an anxious toddler trying to rouse a foully hungover stepfather. So it was that she too came to see me for the feckless nance I so surely was.

'But I'm too English to abuse an animal,' I said in a haughty whine as Marie-Christine poured me out some sort of infusion.

'Maybe you think it is not love, but your relationship will be better if you are strong and take no bullshit,' she replied in mild exasperation. 'Just imagine how it is sometimes with dogs.'

But I have never owned a dog. 'I could tell you how it is sometimes with cats,' I offered, and she shot a quick glance at Hanno. In the name of all that is holy, said the glance, who *is* this baby's arse of a man?

The donkeys came to me again that night, massing snortily

around the caravan as I pursued elusive sleep. A huff led to a puff, then to a bray and within a minute the formica walls around me were shaking to the nostrilled trumpets of a frenzied wind section. Was this a warning to safeguard their diminutive colleague? A hearty *'bon voyage'*? Drawing the covers up to my taut features, I began to understand their dreadful orchestra. They were laughing at me.

THIRTEEN STEPS DOWN

BY RUTH RENDELL

Since her first novel, *From Doon with Death*, was published in 1964, Ruth Rendell has become one of Britain's most celebrated and successful writers. Though best known for the novels and stories featuring Chief Inspector Wexford, she has also published many psychological thrillers both under her own name and that of Barbara Vine. She has won many prizes, and is a multiple winner of both the Gold Dagger awarded by the Crime Writers' Association and the Edgar Allen Poe award from the Mystery Writers of America. She was created a life peer in 1997.

Thirteen Steps Down is, remarkably, her 79th book. It centres on Mix Cellini, a young man obsessed with John Christie, the infamous serial killer of Rillington Place. Cellini is also increasingly fixated upon a celebrity model, Nerissa Nash, who lives within comfortable walking distance of the old and run-down house in Notting Hill where he is the tenant of Gwendolen Chawcer. Miss Chawcer is an elderly and reclusive woman who reads voraciously and constantly returns to memories of the doctor whom she last saw some fifty years ago. Cellini's progressively more desperate and deluded attempts to insert himself into Nash's life veer abruptly into murderous violence. As his fantasies collide with an uncooperative and unpredictable reality, these two interconnected stories move inexorably to their disturbing climax.

Ruth Rendell's new novel exhibits many recognizable trademarks: the exhaustive knowledge and intricate use of

London as an atmospheric backdrop; her exploration of the psychological oddities and obsessions which underlie the surface normalities of individual lives; the unsettling use of domestic detail; and the processes by which everyday structures of routine and habit unravel into devastating and unforeseen disorder. It powerfully conveys her understanding of the ways in which violence and murder are rooted, and grow with alarming force and speed, in outwardly ordinary lives.

Recommended by Naomi Nile,
Waterstone's Bristol University

£16.99
ISBN: 0091799759
Published October 2004

Mix was standing where the street should have been. Or where he thought it should have been. By this time shock and disbelief were past. Bitter disappointment, then rage, filled his body and climbed into his throat, half-choking him. How dared they? How could they, whoever they were, destroy what should have been a national monument? The house itself should have been a museum, one of those blue plaques high up on its wall, the garden, lovingly preserved just as it was, part of a tour visiting parties could have made. If they had wanted a curator they need have looked no further than him.

Everything was new, carefully and soullessly designed. 'Soulless' – that was the word and he was proud of himself for thinking it up. The place was *pretty*, he thought in disgust, typical yuppie-land building. The petunias in the flowerbeds particularly enraged him. Of course he knew that sometime back before he was born they had changed the name from Rillington Place to Ruston Close but now there wasn't even a Ruston Close any more. He had brought an old map with him but it was useless, harder to find the old streets than searching for the child's features in the fifty-year-old face. Fifty years was right. It would be half a century since Reggie was caught and hanged. If they had to rename the streets, surely they could have put up a sign somewhere which said, *Formerly Rillington Place*. Or something to tell visitors they were in

Reggie country. Hundreds must come here, some of them expectant and deeply disappointed, others knowing nothing of the place's history, all of them encountering this smart little enclave of red brick and raised flowerbeds, geraniums and busy lizzies spilling out of window boxes and trees chosen for their golden and creamy white foliage.

It was midsummer and a fine day, the sky a cloudless blue. The little grass plots were a bright and lush green, a pink climbing plant draping a rosy cloak over walls cunningly constructed on varying levels. Mix turned away, the choking anger making his heart beat faster and more loudly, thud, thud, thud. If he had known everything had been eradicated, he would never have considered the flat in St Blaise House. He had come to this corner of Notting Hill solely because it had been Reggie's district. Of course he had known the house itself was gone and its neighbours too but still he had been confident the place would be easily recognizable, a street shunned by the faint-hearted, frequented by intelligent enthusiasts like himself. But the feeble, the squeamish, the politically correct had had their way and torn it all down. They would have been laughing at the likes of him, he thought, and triumphant at replacing history with a tasteless housing estate.

The visit itself he had been saving up as a treat for when he was settled in. A treat! How often, when he was a child, had a promised treat turned into a let-down? Too often, he seemed to remember, and it didn't stop when one was grown-up and a responsible person. Still, he wasn't moving again, not after paying Ed and his mate to paint the place and re-fit the kitchen. He turned his back on the pretty little new houses, the trees and flowerbeds, and walked slowly up Oxford Gardens and across Ladbroke Grove to view the house where Reggie's first victim had had a room. At least that wasn't changed. By the look of it, no one had painted it since the woman's death in 1943. No one seemed to know which room it had been, there were no details in any of the books he'd read. He gazed at the windows, speculating and making guesses, until someone looked out of one of them and he thought he'd better move on.

St Blaise Gardens was quite up-market where it crossed Oxford Gardens, tree-lined with ornamental cherries, but the further he walked downhill it too went down until it was all sixties local authority housing, dry cleaners and motorcycle spare parts places and corner shops. All except for the terrace on the other side, isolated elegant Victorian, and the big house, the only one like it in the whole neighbourhood that wasn't divided into a dozen flats, St Blaise House. Pity they hadn't pulled that lot down, Mix thought, and left Rillington Place alone.

No cherries here but great dusty plane trees with huge leaves and bark peeling off their trunks. They were partly responsible for making the place so dark. He paused to look at the house, marvelling at its size, as he always did, and wondering why on earth the old woman hadn't sold it to a developer years ago.

Three floors high, it was of once-white, now grey, stucco, with steps up to a great front door that was half-hidden in the depths of a pillared portico. Above, almost under the eaves, was a circular window quite different from the other oblong windows, being of stained glass, clouded by the accumulation of grime built up over the years since it had last been cleaned.

Mix let himself in. The hallway alone, he had thought when he first saw the place, was big enough for a normal size flat to fit inside, big, square and dark like everything in there. Big dark chairs with carved backs stood uselessly against the walls, one of them under a huge mirror in the carved wooden frame, its glass all spotted with greenish blots like islands on a map of the sea. Stairs went down to a basement but he had never been in it and as far as he knew no one else had for years and years.

When he came in he always hoped she wouldn't be anywhere about and usually she wasn't, but today he was out of luck. Dressed in her usual garments, long droopy cardigan and skirt with a dipping hemline, she was standing beside a huge carved table which must have weighed a ton, holding up a coloured flier advertising a Tibetan restaurant. When she saw him she said, 'Good afternoon, Mr Cellini,' in her upper-class drawl, putting, he thought, a lot of scorn into her voice.

When he spoke to Gwendolen Chawcer, when addressing her was unavoidable, he did his best to shock her – so far without marked success.

'You'll never guess where I've been.'

'That is almost a certainty,' she said. 'So it seems pointless to attempt it.'

Sarcastic old bitch. 'Rillington Place,' he said, 'or where it used to be. I wanted to see where Christie buried all those women he killed in his garden but there's not a trace of it left.'

She put the flier back on the table. No doubt, it would lie there for months. Then she surprised him. 'I went to his house once,' she said, 'when I was young.'

'You did? Why was that?'

He knew she wouldn't be forthcoming and she wasn't. 'I had a reason to go there. The visit lasted no more than half an hour. He was an unpleasant man.'

He couldn't control his excitement. 'What sort of an impression did he make on you? Did you feel you were in the presence of a murderer? Was his wife there?'

She laughed her cold laugh. 'Goodness, Mr Cellini, I've no time to answer all these questions. I have to get on.'

With what? She seldom did anything but read, as far as he knew. She must have read thousands of books, she was always at it. He felt frustrated after her unsatisfactory but provocative response. She might be a mine of information about Reggie but she was too standoffish to talk about it.

He began to mount the stairs, hating them with a fierce hatred, though they were not narrow or precarious or winding. There were fifty-two and one of the things he disliked about them was that they were composed of three flights, twenty-two in this stretch, seventeen in the next, but thirteen in the top flight. If there was anything which upset Mix more than unpleasant surprises and rude old women, it was the number thirteen. St Blaise House, fortunately, was number 54 St Blaise Avenue.

One day when old Chawcer was out he had counted the bedrooms, not including his own, and found there were nine. Some were furnished, if you could call it furniture, some were not. The whole place was filthy. In his opinion, no one had done any housework in it for years, though he had seen her flicking about with a feather duster. All that woodwork, carved with shields and swords and helmets, faces and flowers, leaves and garlands and ribbons, lay under an ancient accumulation of dust. Banister was linked to banister and cornice to picture rail by ropes of cobwebs. She had lived here all her long life, first with her parents, then with her dad, then alone. Apart from that he knew nothing about her. He didn't even know how she happened to have three bedrooms on the top floor already converted into a flat.

The stairs grew narrower after the first landing and the last flight, the top one, was tiled, not carpeted. Mix had never seen a staircase of shiny black tiles before but there were many things in Miss Chawcer's house he had never seen before. No matter what kind of shoes he wore, those tiles made a terrible noise, a thump-thumping or a clack-clacking, and his belief was that she had tiled the stairs so that she would be able to tell what time her tenant came in. He had already got into the habit of removing his shoes and continuing in his socks alone. It wasn't that he ever did anything *wrong* but he didn't want her knowing his business.

The stained glass window speckled the top landing with spots of coloured light. It was a picture of a girl looking into a pot with some sort of plant in it. When old Chawcer brought him up here for the first time she had called it the Isabella window and the picture Isabella and the Pot of Basil, which made very little sense to Mix. As far as he was concerned, basil was something growing in a bag you bought at Tesco. The girl looked ill, her face was the only bit of the glass that was white, and Mix resented having to see her each time he went into, or came out of, his flat.

He called his home an apartment but Gwendolen Chawcer called it 'rooms.' She lived in the past, in his opinion, and not thirty or forty years ago like most old people but a hundred years. He had put in the bathroom himself with Ed's and his mate's help and fitted the kitchen. He paid for it, so Miss Chawcer couldn't really complain. She ought to have been pleased; it would still be there for the next tenant when he was famous and had moved out. The fact was that she had never been able to see the need for a bathroom. When she was young, she told him, you had a chamber pot in your bedroom and a basin on the washstand and the maid brought you up a jug of hot water.

Mix had a bedroom as well and a large living room, dominated by a huge poster photograph of Nerissa Nash, taken when a newspaper started naming the models as well as the clothes designers. That was in the days when they called her the poor man's Naomi Campbell. They did so no longer. Mix stood in front of the poster, as he often did when he first came in, like a religious contemplating a holy picture, his lips murmuring, 'I love you, I adore you,' instead of prayers.

*

He was earning good money at Fiterama and he had spent freely on this flat. The chrome-encased television, video and DVD player were on the hire purchase as was most of the kitchen equipment but that, to use one of Ed's favourite expressions, was par for the course, everyone did it. He had paid for the white carpet and grey tweed suite with ready cash, buying the black marble statue of the nude girl on an impulse but not for a moment regretting his purchase. The poster of Nerissa he had had framed in the same chrome finish as the TV. In the black ash shelving he kept his collection of Reggie books: *10 Rillington Place*, *John Reginald Halliday Christie*, *The Christie Legend*, *Murder in Rillington Place* and *Christie's Victims* among many others. Richard Attenborough's film of *10 Rillington Place* he had on video and DVD. It was outrageous, he thought, that one Hollywood movie after another was remade while you never heard a thing about a re-make of that. The one he possessed he often played and the digital version was even better, clearer and brighter. Richard Attenborough was wonderful, he wasn't arguing about that, but he didn't look much like Reggie. A taller actor was needed with sharper features and burning eyes.

Mix was inclined to day-dream and sometimes he speculated as to whether he would be famous through knowing Nerissa or through his expert knowledge of Reggie. There was probably no one alive today, not even Ludovic Kennedy who had written *the* book, who knew more. It might be his mission in life to reawaken interest in Rillington Place and its most famous occupant, though how this was to come about after what he had seen that afternoon, was as yet a mystery. He would solve it, of course. Perhaps he would write a book about Reggie himself, and not one full of feeble comments on the man's wickedness and depravity. His book would draw attention to the murderer as artist.

It was getting on for six. Mix poured himself his favourite drink. He had invented it himself and called it Boot Camp because it had such a savage kick. It mystified him that no one he had offered it to seemed to share his taste for a double measure of vodka, a glass of sauvignon and a tablespoonful of Cointreau poured over crushed ice. His fridge was the kind which spewed out the crushed ice all prepared. He was just savouring the first sip when his mobile rang.

It was Colette Gilbert-Bamber to tell him she was desperate to get her treadmill repaired. It might be no more than the electric plug or it might be something bigger. Her husband had gone out but she had had to stay at home because she was expecting an important phone call. Mix knew what all that meant. Being in love with his distant star, his queen and lady, didn't mean he was never to treat himself to a bit of fun. Once he and Nerissa were together, a recognized item, it would be a different thing.

Regretfully but getting his priorities right, Mix put his Boot Camp into the fridge. He cleaned his teeth, gargled with a mouthwash which tasted not unlike his cocktail without the stimulus, and made his way down the stairs. In the midst of the house you wouldn't have guessed how fine the day was and bright and hot the sunshine. Here it was always cold and strangely silent too, it always was. You couldn't hear the

Metropolitan Line running above ground from Latimer Road to Shepherd's Bush, or the traffic in Ladbroke Grove. The only noise came from the Westway but if you didn't know you wouldn't have imagined you were listening to traffic. It sounded like the sea, like waves breaking on the shore, or what you hear when you hold a big seashell up to your ear, a soft unceasing roar.

*

These days Gwendolen sometimes needed the help of a magnifying glass to read small print. And, unfortunately, most of the books she wanted to read were printed in what she understood to be called 10-point. Her ordinary glasses couldn't cope with papa's edition of *The Decline and Fall of the Roman Empire*, for instance, or what she was reading now, a very old copy of *Middlemarch*, published in the nineteenth century.

Like her bedroom above it, the drawing room encompassed the whole depth of the house, a pair of large sash windows overlooking the street, French windows at the back, giving on to the garden. When she was reading Gwendolen reclined on a sofa upholstered in dark brown corduroy, its back surmounted with a carved mahogany dragon. The dragon's tail curved round to meet one of the sofa arms, while its head reared up as it snarled at the black marble fireplace. Most of the furniture was rather like that, carved and thickly padded and covered in velvet which was brown or dull green or the dark red of claret, but some was made of dark veined marble with gilt legs. There was a very large mirror on one wall, framed in gilt leaves and fruit and curlicues, which had grown dull with time and lack of care.

Beyond the French windows, open now to the warm evening light, lay the garden. Gwendolen still saw it as it used to be, the lawn closely mown to the smoothness of emerald velvet, the herbaceous border alight with flowers, the trees pruned to make the best of their luxuriant foliage. Or, rather, she saw that it could be like that with a little attention, nothing that couldn't be achieved by a day's work. That the grass was knee-high, the flowerbeds a mass of weeds and the trees ruined by dead branches, escaped her notice. The printed word was more real to her than a comfortable interior and pleasing exterior.

Her mind and her memories too were occasionally stronger than the book; then she laid it down to stare at the brownish cobweb-hung ceiling and the dusty prisms on the chandelier, to think and to remember.

The man Cellini she disliked but that was of small importance. His inelegant conversation had awakened sleeping things, Christie and his murders, Rillington Place, her fear, Dr Reeves and Bertha. It must be at least fifty-two years ago, maybe fifty-three. Rillington Place had been a sordid slum, the terraces of houses with front doors opening on to the street, an iron foundry with a tall chimney at the far end of it. Until she went there she had no idea such places existed. She had led a sheltered life, both before that day and after it. Bertha would have married – those sort of people always did. Probably had a string of children who by now would be middle-aged, the first one of them the cause of her misfortunes.

Why did women behave like that? She had never understood. She had never been tempted. Not even with Dr Reeves. Her feelings for him had always been chaste and honourable, as had his for her. She was sure of that, in spite of his subsequent behaviour. Perhaps, after all, she had chosen the better part. Like that girl in Wordsworth's poem, she had 'dwelt among the untrodden ways,' and none the worse for that.

What on earth made Cellini so interested in Christie? It wasn't a healthy attitude of mind. Gwendolen picked up her book again. Not in this one but in another of George Eliot's, *Adam Bede*, there was a girl who had behaved like Bertha and met a dreadful fate. She read for another half-hour, lost to the world, oblivious to everything but the page in front of her. A footfall above her head alerted her.

Poor as her sight was becoming, Gwendolen's hearing was superb. Not for a woman of her age but for anyone of any age. Her friend Olive Fordyce said she was sure Gwendolen could hear a bat squeak. She listened now. He was coming down the stairs. No doubt he thought she didn't know he took his shoes off in an attempt to come and go secretly. She was not so easily deceived. The lowest flight creaked. Nothing he could do would put a stop to that, she thought triumphantly. She heard him padding across the hall but when he closed the front door it was with a slam which shook the house and caused a whitish flake to drop off the ceiling on to her left foot.

She went to the one of the front windows and saw him getting into his car. It was a small blue car and, in her opinion, he kept it absurdly clean. When he had gone she went out to the kitchen, opened the door on an ancient and never-used spin dryer to take out a netting bag which had once held potatoes. The bag was full of keys. No labels were attached to them but she knew very well the shape and colour of the one she wanted. The key in the pocket of her cardigan, she began to mount the stairs.

It was a long way up but she was used to it. She might be over eighty but she was thin and strong. Never in her life had she had a day's illness. Of course she couldn't climb those stairs as fast as she could fifty years ago but that was only to be expected. Otto was sitting halfway up the top flight, dismembering and eating some small mammal. She took no notice of him nor he of her. The evening sun blazed through the Isabella window and since there was no wind to blow on the glass, a nearly perfect coloured picture of the girl and the pot of basil appeared reflected on the floor, a circular mosaic of reds and blues and purples and greens. Gwendolen stopped to admire it. Rarely indeed was this facsimile so clear and still.

She lingered for only a minute or two before inserting her key in the lock and letting herself into Cellini's flat.

All this white paint was unwise, she thought. It showed every mark. And grey was a bad furnishing colour, cold and stark. She walked into his bedroom, wondering why he bothered to make his bed when he would only have to unmake it at night. Everything was depressingly tidy. Very likely he suffered from that affliction she had read about in a newspaper, Obsessive Compulsive Disorder. The kitchen was just as bad. It looked like one of those on show at the Ideal Home Exhibition, to which Olive had insisted on taking her sometime in the eighties. A place for everything and everything in its place, not a packet or tin left on the counter, nothing in the sink. How could anyone live like that?

She opened the door of the fridge. There was very little food to be seen but in the door rack were two bottles of wine and, in the very front of the middle shelf a nearly full glass of something that looked like faintly coloured water. Gwendolen sniffed it. Not water, certainly not. So he drank, did he? She couldn't say she was surprised. Making her way back into the living room, she stopped at the bookshelves. Any books, no matter of what kind, always drew her attention. These were not the sort she would read, perhaps that anyone should read. All of them, except for one called *Sex for Men in the 21st Century*, was about Christie. She had scarcely thought about the man for more than forty years and today she seemed not to be able to get away from him.

As for Cellini, this would be another of his obsessions. The more I know people, said Gwendolen, quoting her father, the more I like books. She went downstairs and into the kitchen. There she fetched herself a cheese and pickle sandwich, ready-made from the corner shop, and taking it and a glass of orange juice back to the dragon sofa, she returned to *Middlemarch*.

INDELIBLE

BY KARIN SLAUGHTER

Karin Slaughter has never been far away from the bestsellers chart ever since she stormed into them with her frighteningly good first novel *Blindsighted*. Her fourth book *Indelible* includes all her readers' favourite characters: Jeffrey Tolliver, chief-of-police, handsome and level-headed and still in love with his ex-wife Sara Linton (the town's paediatrician and medical examiner); Lena Adams, the feisty female cop with a huge chip on her shoulder; and her police partner, the stalwart and dependable Detective Frank Wallace.

As usual Slaughter grabs you from page one. A violent hostage situation at the police station puts Lena to the test on her first day back on duty after a long leave of absence. What is the connection between Tolliver and the hostage-takers? Could a case of mistaken identity save his life, or has his past finally caught up with him?

Indelible fluidly interchanges from the present hostage situation to the past, when Sara and Jeffrey took a trip to his hometown, after they had been dating for a few months. Sara has to contend with Jeffrey's acerbic and alcoholic mother, his old school friends and past girlfriends. An incident involving Jeffrey's best friend puts an end to the holiday plans, and Sara's professional skills are called upon as things become more sinister. Is the town talk just idle gossip, or is there something about Jeffrey's high school days that Sara needs to know?

The narrative flows with ease, as all the loose ends are pulled together to form an eagerly anticipated and satisfying ending. Karin Slaughter's crime writing is as gritty as Grisham's, her characters as real as Reichs', and her story lines as cleverly crafted as Cornwell's. She produces constant nail-biting, page-turning, up-all-night thrillers and fans certainly won't be disappointed with 'Indelible' – rookies what are you waiting for?

Recommended by Emma Pickering,
Waterstone's Scarborough

£12.99
ISBN: 1844133702
Published August 2004

8:55 A.M.

"Well, look what the cat dragged in," Marla Simms bellowed, giving Sara a pointed look over her silver-rimmed bifocals. The secretary for the police station held a magazine in her arthritic hands, but she set it aside, indicating she had plenty of time to talk.

Sara forced some cheer into her voice, though she had purposefully timed her visit for Marla's coffee break. "Hey, Marla. How're you doing?"

The old woman stared for a beat, a tinge of disapproval putting a crease in her naturally down-turned lips. Sara forced herself not to squirm. Marla had taught the children's Sunday school class at the Primitive Baptist from the day they opened the front doors, and she could still put the fear of God into anyone in town who'd been born after 1952.

She kept her eyes locked on Sara. "Haven't seen you around here in a while."

"Hm," Sara offered, glancing over Marla's shoulder, trying to see into Jeffrey's office. His door was open but he was not behind his desk. The squad room was empty, which meant he was probably in the back. Sara knew she should just walk behind the counter and find him herself—she had done it hundreds of times before—but survivor's instinct kept her from crossing that bridge without first paying the troll.

Marla sat back in her chair, her arms folded. "Nice day out," she said, her tone still casual.

Sara glanced out the door at Main Street, where heat made the asphalt look wavy. The air this morning was humid enough to open every pore on her body. "Sure is."

"And don't you look pretty this morning," Marla continued, indicating the linen dress Sara had chosen after going through nearly every item of clothing in her closet. "What's the occasion?"

"Nothing special," Sara lied. Before she knew what she was doing, she started to fidget with her briefcase, shifting from one foot to the other like she was four instead of nearly forty.

A glimmer of victory flashed in the older woman's eyes. She drew out the silence a bit more before asking, "How's your mama and them?"

"Good," Sara answered, trying not to sound too circumspect. She wasn't naive enough to believe that her private life was no one else's business—in a county as small as Grant, Sara could barely sneeze without the phone ringing from up the street with a helpful "Bless you"—but she would be damned if she'd make it easy for them to gather their information.

"And your sister?"

Sara was about to respond when Brad Stephens saved her by tripping through the front door. The young patrolman caught himself before he fell flat on his face, but the momentum popped his hat off his head and onto the floor at Sara's feet. His gun belt and nightstick flopped under his arms like extra appendages. Behind him, a gaggle of prepubescent children squawked with laughter at his less-than-graceful entrance.

"Oh," Brad said, looking at Sara, then back to the kids, then at Sara again. He picked up his hat, brushing it off with more care than was warranted. She imagined he could not decide which was more embarrassing: eight ten-year-olds laughing at his clumsiness or his former pediatrician fighting an obvious smile of amusement.

Apparently, the latter was worse. He turned back to the group, his voice deeper than usual as if to assert some authority. "This, of course, is the station house, where we do

214

business. Police business. Uh, and we're in the lobby now."
Brad glanced at Sara. To call the area where they stood a
lobby was a bit of a stretch. The room was barely ten feet by
eight, with a cement block wall opposite the glass door at the
entrance. A row of photographs showing various squads in
the Grant County police force lined the wall to Sara's right, a
large portrait in the center showing Mac Anders, the only
police officer in the history of the force who had been killed
in the line of duty.

Across from the portrait gallery, Marla stood sentry
behind a tall beige laminate counter that separated visitors
from the squad room. She was not a naturally short woman,
but age had made her so by crooking her body into a nearly
perfect question mark. Her glasses were usually halfway
down the bridge of her nose, and Sara, who wore glasses to
read, was always tempted to push them back up. Not that
Sara would ever do such a thing. For all Marla knew about
everybody and their neighbor—and their dog—in town, not
much was known about her. She was a widow with no
children. Her husband had died in the Second World War.
She had always lived on Hemlock, which was two streets
over from Sara's parents. She knitted and she taught
Sunday school and worked full-time at the station answering
phones and trying to make sense of the mountains of
paperwork. These facts hardly offered great insight into
Marla Simms. Still, Sara always thought there had to be
more to the life of a woman who had lived some eighty-odd
years, even if she'd lived all of them in the same house where
she had been born.

Brad continued his tour of the station, pointing to the large,
open room behind Marla. "Back there's where the detectives
and patrol officers like myself conduct their business . . . calls
and whatnot. Talking to witnesses, writing reports, typing
stuff into the computer, and, uh . . ." His voice trailed off as
he finally noticed he was losing his audience. Most of the
children could barely see over the counter. Even if they could,
thirty empty desks spread out in rows of five with various
sizes of filing cabinets between them were hardly attention-

grabbing. Sara imagined the kids were wishing they had stayed in school today.

Brad tried, "In a few minutes, I'll show y'all the jail where we arrest people. Well, not arrest them," he gave Sara a nervous glance, lest she point out his mistake. "I mean, this is where we take them after we arrest them. Not here, but back in the jail."

Silence fell like a hammer, only to be interrupted by an infectious giggle that started in the back of the group. Sara, who knew most of the children from her practice at the children's clinic, hushed a few with a sharp look. Marla took care of the rest, her swivel chair groaning with relief as she raised herself above the counter. The giggling shut off like a faucet.

Maggie Burgess, a child whose parents gave more credence to her opinion than any child of that age ought to be given, dared to say, "Hey, Dr. Linton," in a grating, singsong voice.

Sara gave a curt nod. "Maggie."

"Uh," Brad began, a deep blush still souring his milk-white complexion. Sara was keenly aware of his gaze lingering a little too long on her bare legs. "Ya'll . . . uh . . . y'all know Dr. Linton."

Maggie rolled her eyes. "Well, *yeah*," she said, her sarcastic tone reviving a few giggles.

Brad pushed on. "Dr. Linton is also the medical examiner in town, in addition to being a pediatrician." He spoke in an instructional tone, though surely the children already knew this. It was a subject of great humor on the bathroom walls at the elementary school. "I imagine she's here on county business. Dr. Linton?"

"Yes," Sara answered, trying to sound like Brad's peer rather than someone who could remember him bursting into tears at the mere mention of a shot. "I'm here to talk to the Chief of Police about a case we're working on."

Maggie opened her mouth again, probably to repeat something horrible she had heard her mother say about Sara and Jeffrey's relationship, but Marla's chair squeaked and the child remained silent. Sara vowed she would go to church next Sunday just to thank the woman.

Marla's voice was only slightly less condescending than Maggie's when she told Sara, "I'll go check-see if Chief Tolliver is available."

"Thank you," Sara answered, promptly changing her mind about church.

"Well, uh . . ." Brad began, brushing off his hat again. "Why don't we go on back now?" He opened one of the swinging doors in the counter to allow the children through, telling Sara, "Ma'am," giving her a polite nod before following them.

Sara walked over to the photographs on the wall, looking at all the familiar faces. Except for her time at college and working at Grady Hospital in Atlanta, Sara had always lived in Grant County. Most of the men on the wall had played poker with her father at one time or another. The rest of them had been deacons at the church when Sara was a child or had policed football games back when she was a teenager and was desperately infatuated with Steve Mann, the captain of the Chess Club. Before Sara moved away to Atlanta, Mac Anders had caught Sara and Steve making out behind the House of Chilidogs. A few weeks later, his squad car rolled six times during a high-speed chase and Mac was dead.

Sara shuddered, a superstitious fear creeping along her skin like the legs of a spider. She moved on to the next picture, which showed the force when Jeffrey first took over the job as police chief. He had just come from Birmingham and everyone had been skeptical about the outsider, especially when he hired Lena Adams, Grant County's first female cop. Sara studied Lena in the group photograph. Her chin was tilted up in defiance and there was a glint of challenge in her eye. There were more than a dozen women patrolling now, but Lena would always be the first. The pressure must have been enormous, though Sara had never thought of Lena as a role model. As a matter of fact, there were several things about the other woman's personality that Sara found abhorrent.

"He said come on back." Marla stood at the swinging doors. "It's sad, isn't it?" she asked, indicating the picture of Mac Anders.

"I was at school when it happened."

"I won't even tell you what they did to that animal that chased him off the road." There was a note of approval in Marla's voice. Sara knew the suspect had been beaten so severely he'd lost an eye. Ben Walker, the police chief at the time, was a very different cop from Jeffrey.

Marla held open the doors for her. "He's back in interrogation doing some paperwork."

"Thank you," Sara said, taking one more look at Mac before walking through.

The station house had been built in the mid-1930s when the cities of Heartsdale, Madison, and Avondale had consolidated their police and fire service into the county. The building had been a feed store co-op, but the city bought it cheap when the last of the local farms went bust. All the character had been drained from the building during the renovation, and not much had been done to help the decor in the decades that followed. The squad room was nothing more than a long rectangle, with Jeffrey's office on one side and the bathroom on the other. Dark fake paneling still reeked of nicotine from before the county's antismoking policy. The drop ceiling looked dingy no matter how many times the inserts were replaced. The tile floor was made of asbestos and Sara always held her breath when she walked over the cracked portion by the bathroom. Even without the tile, she would have held her breath near the bathroom. Nowhere was it more evident that the Grant County police force was still predominantly male than in the squad room's unisex bathroom.

She muscled open the heavy fire door that separated the squad room from the rest of the building. A newer section had been built onto the back of the station fifteen years ago when the mayor had realized they could make some money holding prisoners for nearby overburdened counties. A thirty-cell jail block, a conference room, and the interrogation room had seemed luxurious at the time, but age had done its work and despite a recent fresh coat of paint, the newer areas looked just as worn-down as the old ones.

Sara's heels clicked across the floor as she walked down the long hallway, then stopped outside the interrogation room to straighten her dress and buy herself some time. She had not been this nervous around her ex-husband in a long while, and she hoped it did not show as she entered the room.

Jeffrey sat at a long table, stacks of papers spread over the surface as he took notes on a legal pad. His coat was off, his sleeves rolled up. He did not glance up when she came in, but he must have been watching, because when Sara started to close the door, he said, "Don't."

She put her briefcase on the table and waited for him to look up. He didn't, and she was torn between throwing her briefcase at his head and throwing herself at his feet. While these two conflicting emotions had been par for the course throughout the nearly fifteen years they had known each other, it was usually Jeffrey prostrating himself in front of Sara, not the other way around. After four years of divorce, they had finally fallen back into a relationship. Three months ago, he had asked her to marry him again, and his ego could not abide her rejection, no matter how many times she explained her reasons. They had not seen each other outside of work since, and Sara was running out of ideas.

Withholding an exasperated sigh, she said, "Jeffrey?"

"Just leave the report there," he said, nodding toward an empty corner on the table as he underlined something on the legal pad.

"I thought you might want to go over it."

"Was there anything unusual?" he asked, picking up another stack of papers, still not looking at her.

"I found a map in her lower bowel that leads to buried treasure."

He did not take the bait. "Did you put that in the report?"

"Of course not," she teased. "I'm not splitting that kind of money with the county."

Jeffrey gave her a sharp look that said he didn't appreciate her humor. "That's not very respectful to the deceased."

Sara felt a flash of shame but she tried not to show it. "What's the verdict?"

"Natural causes," Sara told him. "The blood and urine came back clean. There were no remarkable findings during the physical exam. She was ninety-eight years old. She died peacefully in her sleep."

"Good."

Sara watched him write, waiting for him to realize she was not going to leave. He had a beautiful, flowing script, the kind you would never expect from an ex-jock and especially from a cop. Part of her had fallen in love with him the first time she had seen his handwriting.

She shifted from one foot to the other, waiting.

"Sit down," he finally relented, holding out his hand for the report. Sara did as she was told, giving him the slim file.

He scanned her notes. "Pretty straightforward."

"I've already talked to her kids," Sara told him, though "kids" hardly seemed appropriate considering that the woman's youngest child was nearly thirty years older than Sara. "They know they were grasping at straws."

"Good," he repeated, signing off on the last page. He tossed it onto the corner of the table and capped his pen. "Is that all?"

"Mama says hey."

He seemed reluctant when he asked, "How's Tess?"

Sara shrugged, because she wasn't exactly sure how to answer. Her relationship with her sister seemed to be deteriorating as rapidly as her one with Jeffrey. Instead, she asked, "How long are you going to keep this up?"

He purposefully misunderstood her, indicating the paperwork as he spoke. "I've got to have it all done before we go to trial next month."

"That's not what I was talking about and you know it."

"I don't think you have a right to use that tone with me." He sat back in the chair. She could see that he was tired, and his usual easy smile was nowhere to be seen.

She asked, "Are you sleeping okay?"

"Big case," he said, and she wondered if that was really

what was keeping him up at night. "What do you want?"

"Can't we just talk?"

"About what?" He rocked his chair back. When she did not answer, he prompted, "Well?"

"I just want to—"

"What?" he interrupted, his jaw set. "We've talked this through a hundred times. There's not a whole lot more to say."

"I want to see you."

"I told you I'm buried in this case."

"So, when it's over . . .?"

"Sara."

"Jeffrey," she countered. "If you don't want to see me, just say it. Don't use a case as an excuse. We've both been buried deeper than this before and still managed to spend time with each other. As I recall, it's what makes this crap"—she indicated the mounds of paperwork—"bearable."

He dropped his chair with a thud. "I don't see the point."

She gave humor another stab. "Well, the sex, for one."

"I can get that anywhere."

Sara raised an eyebrow, but suppressed the obvious comment. The fact that Jeffrey could and sometimes did get sex anywhere was the reason she had divorced him in the first place.

He picked up his pen to resume writing, but Sara snatched it from his hand. She tried to keep the desperation out of her voice as she asked, "Why do we have to get married again for this to work?"

He looked off to the side, clearly annoyed.

She reminded him, "We were married before and it practically ruined us."

"Yeah," he said. "I remember."

She played her trump card. "You could rent out your house to someone from the college."

He paused a second before asking, "Why would I do that?"

"So you could move in with me."

"And live in sin?"

She laughed. "Since when did you become religious?"

221

"Since your father put the fear of God into me," he shot back, his tone completely devoid of humor. "I want a wife, Sara, not a fuckbuddy."

She felt the cut of his words. "Is that what you think I am?"

"I don't know," he told her, his tone something of an apology. "I'm tired of being tied to that string you just yank when you feel lonely."

She opened her mouth but could not speak.

He shook his head, apologizing. "I didn't mean that."

"You think I'm here making a fool of myself because I'm lonely?"

"I don't know anything right now, except that I've got a lot of work to do." He held out his hand. "Can I have my pen back?"

She gripped it tightly. "I want to be with you."

"You're with me now," he said, reaching over to retrieve his pen.

She put her other hand around his, holding him there. "I miss you," she said. "I miss being with you."

He gave a halfhearted shrug, but did not pull away.

She pressed her lips to his fingers, smelling ink and the oatmeal lotion he used when he thought no one was looking. "I miss your hands."

He kept staring.

She brushed his thumb with her lips. "Don't you miss me?"

He tilted his head to the side, giving another indefinite shrug.

"I want to *be* with you. I want to . . ." She looked over her shoulder again, making certain no one was there. She lowered her voice to barely more than a whisper and offered to do something with him that any self-respecting prostitute would charge double for.

Jeffrey's lips parted, shock registering in his eyes. His hand tightened around hers. "You stopped doing that when we got married."

"Well . . ." She smiled. "We're not married anymore, are we?"

He seemed to be thinking it over when a loud knock came

at the open door. It might as well have been a gunshot from Jeffrey's reaction. He jerked his hand back and stood up.

Frank Wallace, Jeffrey's second in command, said, "Sorry."

Jeffrey let his irritation show, though Sara could not guess if it was for her or Frank's benefit. "What is it?"

Frank glanced at the phone on the wall and stated the obvious. "Your extension's off the hook."

Jeffrey waited.

"Marla told me to tell you there's some kid in the lobby asking for you." He took out his handkerchief and wiped his forehead. "Hey, Sara."

She started to return the greeting but stopped at the sight of him. He looked dead on his feet. "Are you all right?"

Frank put his hand to his stomach, a sour look on his face. "Bad Chinese."

She stood, putting her hand to his cheek. His skin was clammy. "You're probably dehydrated," she told him, putting her fingers to his wrist to check his pulse. "Are you getting enough fluids?"

He shrugged.

She stared at the second hand on her watch. "Throwing up? Diarrhea?"

He shifted uncomfortably over her last question. "I'm okay," he said, but he obviously wasn't. "You look real nice today."

"I'm glad somebody noticed," Sara said, giving Jeffrey a sideways glance.

Jeffrey tapped his fingers on the table, still annoyed. "Go on home, Frank. You look like shit."

Frank's relief was obvious.

Sara added, "If this isn't better tomorrow, call me."

He nodded again, telling Jeffrey, "Don't forget about the kid in the lobby."

"Who is it?"

"Something Smith. I didn't catch . . ." He put a hand to his stomach and made a sick sound. He turned to leave, managing a garbled "Sorry."

Jeffrey waited until Frank was out of earshot to say, "I have to do everything around here."

"He's obviously not well."

"It's Lena's first day back," Jeffrey said, referring to Frank's ex-partner. "She's supposed to be in at ten."

"And?"

"You run into Matt yet? He tried to call in sick, too, but I told him to get his sorry ass in here."

"You think two senior detectives gave themselves food poisoning so they wouldn't have to see Lena?"

Jeffrey walked over to the phone and put the receiver back in the cradle. "I've been here over fifteen years and never seen Matt Hogan eat Chinese."

He had a point, but Sara wanted to give both men the benefit of the doubt. No matter what he said about her, Frank obviously cared for Lena. They had worked together for nearly a decade. Sara knew from personal experience that you could not spend that kind of time with someone and just walk away.

Jeffrey pressed the speaker button, then dialed in an extension. "Marla?"

There was a series of clicking noises as she picked up the receiver. "Yessir?"

"Has Matt shown up yet?"

"Not yet. I'm a little worried what with him being sick and all."

"Tell him I'm looking for him as soon as he walks in the door," Jeffrey ordered. "Is there someone waiting for me?"

She lowered her voice. "Yes. He's kind of impatient."

"I'll be there in a second." He turned the speaker off, mumbling, "I don't have time for this."

"Jeff—"

"I need to see who this is," he said, walking out of the room.

Sara followed him down the hallway, practically running to keep up. "If I break my ankle in these heels . . ."

He glanced down at her shoes. "Did you think you could just waltz in here whoring yourself out and I'd beg you to come back?"

Embarrassment ignited her temper. "Why is it you call it whoring myself out when I *want* to do it, but when I don't want to and I do anyway, all of a sudden it's sexy?"

He stopped at the fire door, resting his hand on the long handle. "That's not fair."

"You think so, too, Dr. Freud?"

"I'm not playing around here, Sara."

"Do you think I am?"

"I don't know what you're doing," he said, and there was a hardness around his eyes that sent a cold chill through her. "I can't keep living like this."

She put her hand on his arm, saying, "Wait." When he stopped, she forced herself to say, "I love you."

He gave her a flippant "Thanks."

"Please," she whispered. "We don't need a piece of paper to tell us how we feel."

"The thing you keep missing," he told her, yanking open the door, "is that I do."

She started to follow him into the squad room, but pride kept her feet rooted to the floor. A handful of patrolmen and detectives were starting their shifts, sitting at their desks as they wrote up reports or made calls. She could see Brad and his group of kids congregating around the coffeemaker, where he was probably regaling them with the brand of filter they used or the number of scoops it took to make a pot.

There were two young men in the lobby, one of them leaning against the back wall, the other standing in front of Marla. Sara took the standing one to be Jeffrey's visitor. Smith was young, probably Brad's age, and dressed in a quilted black jacket that was zipped closed despite the late August heat. His head was shaved and from what she could make of his body under the heavy coat, he was fit and well muscled. He kept scanning the room, his eyes furiously darting around, never resting his gaze on one person for long. He added the front door to his rotation every second time, checking the street. There was definitely something military in his bearing, and for some reason, his general demeanor put Sara on edge.

She looked around the room, taking in what Smith was seeing. Jeffrey had stopped at one of the desks to help a patrolman. He slid his paddle holster to his back as he sat on the edge of the desk and typed something into the computer. Brad was still talking over by the coffeemaker, his hand resting on the top of the mace spray in his belt. She counted five more cops, all of them busy writing reports or entering information into their computers. A sense of danger coursed through Sara's body like a bolt of lightning. Everything in her line of vision became too sharply focused.

The front door made a sucking sound as it opened and Matt Hogan walked in. Marla said, "There you are. We've been waiting for you."

The young man put his hand inside his coat, and Sara screamed, "Jeffrey!"

They all turned to look at her, but Sara was watching Smith. In one fluid motion he pulled out a sawed-off shotgun, pointed it at Matt's face, and squeezed both triggers.

Blood and brain sprayed onto the front door as if from a high-pressure hose. Matt fell back against the glass, the pane cracking straight up the center but not breaking, his face completely blown away. Children started to scream and Brad fell on them en masse, pushing them down to the ground. Gunfire went wild and one of the patrolmen collapsed in front of Sara, a large hole in his chest. His gun discharged on impact, skidding across the floor. Around her, glass flew as family photographs and personal items shot off desks. Computers popped, sending up the acrid smell of burning plastic. Papers floated through the air in a flurry, and the sound of weapons firing was so intense that Sara's ears felt as if they were bleeding.

"Get out!" Jeffrey screamed, just as Sara felt a sharp sting on her face. She put her hand to her cheek where a piece of shrapnel had grazed the flesh. She was kneeling on the floor but could not remember how she had gotten there. She darted behind a filing cabinet, her throat feeling as if she had swallowed acid.

"Go!" Jeffrey was crouched behind a desk, the muzzle of

his gun a constant burst of white as he tried to give her cover. A large boom shook the front of the building, then another.

From behind the fire door, Frank screamed, "This way!" pointing his gun around the jamb, shooting blindly toward the front lobby. A patrolman slammed open the door, exposing Frank as he ran to safety. On the other side of the room, a second cop was shot trying to reach the group of children, his face a mask of pain as he slumped against a filing cabinet. Smoke and the smell of gunpowder filled the air, and still more firepower came from the front lobby. Fear seized Sara as she recognized the snare-drum *tat-tat-tat* of an automatic weapon. The killers had come prepared for a shoot-out.

"Dr. Linton!" someone screamed. Seconds later, Sara felt a pair of small hands clinging to her neck. Maggie Burgess had managed to break loose, and instinctively, Sara wrapped her own body around the girl's. Jeffrey saw this, and he took out his ankle holster, giving Sara the signal to run as soon as he started firing. She slipped off her high heels, waiting for what seemed like hours until Jeffrey raised his head above the desk he was hiding behind and started shooting with both guns. Sara bolted toward the fire door and threw the child to Frank. Floor tiles splintered and exploded in front of her as bullets sprayed, and she backed up on her hands and feet until she was safely behind the filing cabinet again.

Sara's hands moved wildly as she checked to see if she had been shot. There was blood all over her, but she knew it was not her own. Frank cracked open the door again. Bullets popped off the heavy-gauge steel and he returned fire, sticking his hand around the edge and shooting.

"Get out!" Jeffrey repeated, preparing to give her cover, but Sara could see one of her kids from the clinic hiding behind a row of fallen chairs. Ron Carver looked as terrified as she felt, and Sara held up her hands to stop the child from running before a signal from Jeffrey. Without warning, the boy took off toward her, his chin tucked into his chest and his arms pumping as the air exploded around him. Jeffrey started rapid-firing to draw the shooter away, but a stray bullet zinged through the air, practically severing the child's foot.

Ron barely broke stride, using the pulp that was left of his ankle to propel himself forward.

He collapsed into Sara's arms, and she could feel his heart fluttering in his chest like the wings of a small bird as she ripped off his cotton shirt. She tore the material length-wise and used the sleeve to wrap a tight tourniquet. She used the other half of the shirt to tie his foot on, hoping it could be saved.

"Don't make me go out there," the child begged. "Dr. Linton, please don't make me."

Sara made her tone stern. "Ronny, we have to go."

"Please don't make me!" he wailed.

Jeffrey screamed, "Sara!"

Sara scooped the boy close to her body and waited for Jeffrey's signal. It came, and she held Ron tight as she ran in a crouch toward the door.

Halfway there, the boy started to kick and scratch at her in wild panic, shrieking, "No! Don't make me!" at the top of his lungs.

She clamped her hand over his mouth and forced herself toward the door, barely registering the pain as his teeth cut into the flesh of her palm. Frank reached out, snatching Ron by his shirt and yanking him to safety. He tried to grab Sara, too, but she ran back to the filing cabinet, looking for more children. Another bullet whizzed past her, and without thinking, she went farther into the room.

She tried twice to see how many children were with Brad, but with the bullets and chaos all around her, she lost count each time. She searched frantically for Jeffrey. He was about fifteen feet away reloading his gun. Their eyes locked just before his shoulder jerked back, throwing him against the desks. A plant fell to the floor, the pot breaking into a thousand pieces. His body convulsed, his legs gave a violent twitch, and then he was still. With Jeffrey down, everything seemed to stop. Sara darted under the nearest desk, her ears ringing from the gunfire. The room went quiet but for Marla's screaming, her voice trilling up and down like a siren.

"Oh, God," Sara whispered, looking frantically under the

desk. Just over the front counter, she saw Smith standing with a gun in each hand, scanning the room for movement. The other young man was beside him, pointing an assault rifle toward the front door. Smith was wearing a Kevlar vest under the jacket, and she could see two more guns holstered to his chest. The shotgun lay on the counter. Both gunmen were out in the open, but no one fired on them. Sara tried to remember who else was in the room but again could not keep count.

Movement came to her far left. Another shot was fired and there was the ping of a ricochet followed by a low groan. A child's scream was stifled. Sara flattened herself to the floor, trying to see under the other desks. In the far corner, Brad had his arms spread open, keeping the kids down on the floor. They were huddled together, sobbing as one.

The officer who had fallen against the filing cabinets moaned, trying to raise his gun. Sara recognized the man as Barry Fordham, a patrol cop she had danced with at the last policeman's ball.

"Put it down!" Smith screamed. "Put it down!"

Barry tried to raise his gun, but he couldn't control his wrist. His gun flopped wildly in the air. The man with the assault rifle turned slowly toward Barry and fired one shot into the cop's head with frightening precision. The back of Barry's skull banged into the metal cabinet and stuck there. When Sara looked at the second gunman, he had returned to guarding the front door as if nothing had happened.

"Who else?" Smith demanded. "Identify yourself!"

Sara heard someone scramble behind her. She saw a blur of colors as one of the detectives ran into Jeffrey's office. A spray of bullets followed him. Seconds later, the window was broken out.

"Stay where you are!" Smith ordered. "Everyone stay where you are!"

A child's scream came from Jeffrey's office, followed by more shattered glass. Remarkably, the window between the office and the squad room had not been broken. Smith broke it now with a single shot.

Sara cringed as the huge shards of glass splintered against the floor.

"Who else is here?" Smith demanded, and she heard the shotgun being cracked and loaded. "Show your face or I'll kill this old lady, too!"

Marla's scream was cut off by a slap.

Sara finally found Jeffrey near the center of the room. She could only see his right shoulder and arm. He was lying on his back. His body was motionless. Blood pooled around him and his hand held his gun at his side, the grip relaxed. He was five desks away on the diagonal, but she could still see the band of his Auburn class ring on his finger.

A hushed "Sara" came from her right. Frank was crouched behind the steel fire door, his weapon drawn. He motioned for her to crawl back toward him, but Sara shook her head. His voice was an angry hiss as he repeated, "Sara."

She looked at Jeffrey again, willing him to move, to show some signs of life. The remaining children were still huddled with Brad, their sobs slowly stifled by fear. She could not leave any of them and she told this to Frank with another sharp shake of her head. She ignored his angry snort of breath.

"Who's left?" Smith demanded. "Show yourself or I'm gonna shoot this old bitch!" Marla screamed, but Smith screamed louder. "Who's fucking back there?"

Sara was about to respond when Brad said, "Over here."

Before she could let herself think, Sara ran in a crouch toward the closest desk, hoping Smith was looking at Brad. She held her breath, waiting to be shot.

"Where're those kids?" Smith demanded.

Brad's voice was amazingly calm. "We're over here. Don't shoot. It's just me and three little girls left. We're not gonna do anything."

"Stand up."

"I can't, man. I gotta take care of these kids."

Marla cried, "Please don't—" and her words were cut off by another slap.

Sara closed her eyes for a second, thinking about her family, about all that had been left unsaid between them. Then she pushed them out of her mind and instead thought about the children left in the room. She stared at the gun in Jeffrey's hand, pinning everything on the weapon. If she could get to Jeffrey's gun, maybe they would have a chance. Four more desks. Jeffrey was only four more desks away. She let herself look at him again. His body was still, his hand unmoving.

Smith was still focused on Brad. "Where's your gun?"

"It's here," Brad said, and Sara darted toward the next desk, overshooting it but managing to stop short behind a lateral filing cabinet. "I gotta bunch of little girls here, man. I'm not going to draw on you. I haven't touched my gun."

"Throw it over here."

Sara held her breath and waited until she heard Brad's gun sliding across the floor before she ran to the next desk.

"Don't move!" Smith screamed as Sara skidded to a stop behind the desk. Her feet were sweating, and she saw her own bloody footprints tracing her route across the floor. She stumbled, but caught herself before she fell into the open.

Marla wailed, "Please!"

There was the loud retort of flesh against flesh. Marla's chair gave a god-awful groan, as if it had snapped in two. Sara watched under the desk as Marla's body slammed into the ground. Saliva spurted from her mouth and her teeth slid across the tiles.

"I told you not to move!" Smith repeated, giving Marla's chair a vicious kick that sent it spinning into the wall.

Sara tried to control her breathing as she moved closer to Jeffrey. One desk stood between them, but it was turned the wrong way, blocking her path. She would be in Smith's line of fire if she ran. She was almost directly across from the children. They were three desks away. She could get the gun and . . . Sara felt her heart stop. What could she do with the gun? What could she accomplish that nearly ten cops could not?

Surprise, Sara thought. She had surprise. Smith and his accomplice did not know that she was in the room. She would surprise them.

"Where's your backup?" Smith demanded.

"I'm patrol. I don't carry a second—"

"Don't lie to me!" He fired in Brad's direction and instead of the screams Sara expected, there was silence. She looked back under the desks, trying to see if anyone had been shot. Three sets of glassy eyes stared back. Shock had taken over. The girls were too afraid to scream.

Silence filled the room like a poisonous gas. Sara counted to thirty-one before Smith asked, "You still there, man?"

She put her hand to her chest, scared her heart was beating too loudly. From what she could see of Brad, he was not moving. Her mind flashed on an image of him sitting there, his arms still around the children, his head gone. She squeezed her eyes shut, trying to force the image from her brain.

She chanced another look at Smith, who was standing where Marla had greeted her less than ten minutes ago. He had a nine-millimeter in one hand and the shotgun in another. His jacket was open and Sara could see two empty holsters along with extra shells for the shotgun strapped to his chest. Another pistol was tucked into the front of his jeans and at his feet was a long black duffel bag that probably contained more ammunition. The second gunman was behind the counter, his weapon still pointing toward the front door. His body was tensed, his finger resting to the side of the trigger on his rifle. He was chewing gum, and Sara found his silent gum-chewing more unnerving than Smith's threats.

Smith repeated, "You there, man?" He paused before trying again. "You there?"

Finally, Brad said, "I'm here."

Sara let out a slow breath, relief weakening her muscles. She flattened herself to the floor, knowing the best way to get to Jeffrey would be to slide past a row of overturned filing cabinets. Slowly, she made her way along the cold tiles, reaching her hand out toward his. The tips of her fingers finally grazed the cuff of his jacket. She closed her eyes, inching closer.

The gun in his hand was spent, though Sara could have guessed as much if she had let herself think about it. Jeffrey had been reloading when he was shot, and the magazine had dropped to the floor, splitting on impact. Bullets were everywhere—useless, unused bullets. She shouldn't be surprised by that, just like she shouldn't be surprised to feel the coldness of his skin or, when her fingers finally rested upon his wrist, the absence of his pulse.